THE HIDDEN LEGACY of
WORLD WAR II
A DAUGHTER'S JOURNEY OF DISCOVERY

CAROL SCHULTZ VENTO

FOREWORDS BY
THOMAS CHILDERS AND CHRISTEN HARTY SCHAEFFER

SUNBURY
PRESS®
Mechanicsburg, PA USA

Published by Sunbury Press, Inc.
Mechanicsburg, PA USA

SUNBURY
PRESS®

www.sunburypress.com

For information about special discounts for bulk purchases, please contact Sunbury Press Orders Dept. at (855) 338-8359 or orders@sunburypress.com.

To request one of our authors for speaking engagements or book signings, please contact Sunbury Press Publicity Dept. at publicity@sunburypress.com.

SECOND SUNBURY PRESS EDITION: June 2024

Set in Adobe Garamond Pro | Interior design by Crystal Devine | Cover by Lawrence Knorr | Edited by Lawrence Knorr.

Publisher's Cataloging-in-Publication Data
Names: Vento, Carol Schultz, author.
Title: The hidden legacy of World War II : a daughter's journey of discovery / Carol Schultz Vento.
Description: Second trade paperback edition. | Mechanicsburg, PA : Sunbury Press, 2024.
Summary: Carol Schultz Vento recounts the post-World War II years of her famous father, Arthur "Dutch" Schultz.
Identifiers: ISBN : 979-8-88819-193-4 (paperback) | ISBN : 979-8-88819-194-1 (ePub).
Subjects: BIOGRAPHY & AUTOBIOGRAPHY / Military | HISTORY / Wars & Conflicts / World War II / European Theater | PSYCHOLOGY / Psychopathology / Post-Traumatic Stress Disorder (PTSD).

Designed in the USA
0 1 1 2 3 5 8 13 21 34 55

For the Love of Books!

For my sister,
Rosemary Schultz (b.1951 – d.1973)
who walked part of this path with me.
There is sadness that we could not
complete this journey together.

CONTENTS

CONTENTS

ACKNOWLEDGMENTS

For my community of friends, near and far away, I truly appreciate your words of support.

Special thanks to:

Nancy Bowker, my longtime friend and fellow writer who has encouraged me since the moment we met in that writing class.

Ilene Baker, friend and co-creator of the Daughters of D-Day Facebook page, who shares my passion for finding our fathers' hidden World War II stories and whose skill enabled us to reach others to create a community of World War II children.

My daughter, Rosemary Vento Shea for her invaluable insights and support and my son-in-law Michael Shea for his much appreciated help.

My husband, Frank, for his love and support and for discovering multiple and important sources of information and always listening to my interminable discussions of the after effects of war.

My late stepfather, Lee Bondy, for his years of constant support, love and steadfastness.

My late mother, Madeline Bondy, for her love and belief in me and for helping me understand the reality of my father's invisible wounds of war.

My late father, Arthur Dutch Schultz, for being a role model of bravery and for teaching this paratrooper daughter to always soldier on in the face of adversity.

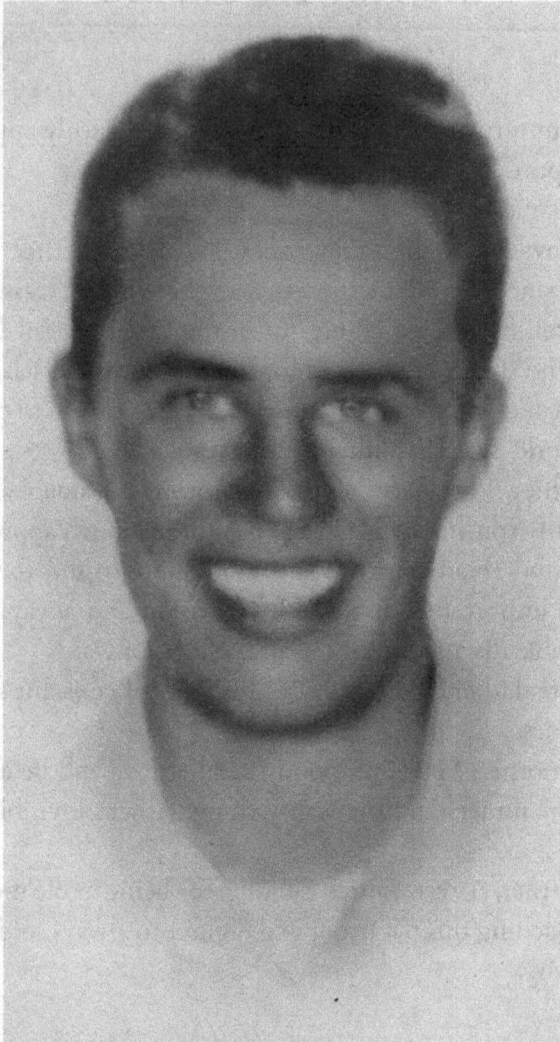

Dutch before World War II (back cover image)

AUTHOR'S NOTE

This is a war story of sorts. The two men who had a major influence on my life were World War II veterans. My late father, Arthur 'Dutch' Schultz, fought in battles that have appeared in films and military history books about paratroopers in the European Theater. Lee Bondy, my step-father, saw duty as a radar technician on the Cleveland, a light cruiser in the Pacific. While there is some description of the fighting history of my father and stepfather in this book, my main focus is on the homecoming. Over sixteen million people, more than twelve percent of the American population at the time, served in World War II—416,837 did not come home alive, and as of 2024, the remains of 72,000 have never been recovered. Some of the men who lost their lives were parents, leaving 183,000 children fatherless—670,846 returned with physical wounds, but what has never been accurately counted are those who came home with broken spirits—the invisible wounds of war.

My father and stepfather both saw combat in WWII, my Dad as part of the 82nd Airborne's 505th Parachute Infantry Regiment, and my stepDad, Lee, on a Naval fighting ship, but they did not both carry war trauma back on the ships with them.

For the entirety of his life, my father struggled with the remnants of World War II, a war that brought him glory and honor but also cost him dearly. Dad was resilient and somehow managed to fight the demons and use what he had learned from his struggles to help others with their demons, but he was never totally free. While my stepDad's story of successful reentry into society and his smoother path through life is much more well-known in the popularized narrative of the Greatest Generation, my book attempts to fill the void in the narrative—the combat soldiers whose struggles are strikingly similar to the later battles with Post-traumatic Stress Disorder experienced by veterans of America's subsequent wars.

My father wanted this story to be told. In 2003, when I said that I wanted to write a book about his war, he told me, "Tell your story instead. Say what it was like to grow up with a combat veteran of World War II. And tell the truth." He reiterated that statement shortly before he died in 2005, when my friend, Ilene Baker, and I traveled 3,000 miles cross country to California, where he lived with his latest wife, in order to move my father from a substandard rehabilitation center to a hospital, where he would hopefully find peace in his final days. When we showed him the front page of our newly launched website, Daughters of D-Day, he smiled broadly.

My objective in telling the hidden story of some World War II combat veterans' homecoming stems not from a desire to be a revisionist but rather from a desire to provide a more complete rendering of postwar history. In that, I have allowed my father's words to be my guide. In a 1995 letter to Stephen Ambrose, referring to material Ambrose had requested of my father for inclusion in Ambrose's *Citizen Soldiers,* Dutch Schultz wrote this:[1]

> A couple of my WWII buddies think I should have "left sleeping dogs lie" concerning my stories about our treatment of prisoners. My argument that war corrupts all of us, not just the enemy, doesn't seem to make the point. I understand where they are coming from: they feel that I'm besmirching the honor and reputation of our outfit, and God only know [*sic*] that this was not my intention. My interest is the truth; however it come outs [*sic*]. It's also understanding that combat against the enemy is not the only measure of courage and honor. Equally critical is how the individual soldier fights his own internal struggle between choices of right and wrong.

---

1. A copy of the letter from Ambrose's archive is on the next page.

9 April 1995

Stephen Ambrose
Eisenhower Center
Metropolitan College
University of New Orleans
New Orleans, Louisiana 70148

Dear Mr. Ambrose:

Thank you for your kind remarks regarding my Bulge and Elbe
histories. It made my day!

On 16 March, I sent you the rest of my Normandy history, my
Holland history, two addenda to my Battle of the Bulge history,
and my Rhine River history. I wonder if you have had a chance
to review them?

My reason for asking the question is the a couple of my WWII
buddies think that I should have "left sleeping dogs lie"
concerning my stories about our treatment of prisoners. My
argument that war corrupts all of us, not just the enemy doesn't
seem to make the point. I understand where they are coming
from; they feel that I'm besmirching the honor and reputation
of our outfit, and God only know that this was not my intention.
My interest is the truth; however it come outs. It's also
understanding that combat against the enemy is not the only
measure of courage and honor. Equally critical is how the
individual soldier fights his own internal struggle between
choices of right and wrong.

I get very upset when friends accuse me of being a revisionist,
but hopefully I'll stay the course. Whatever you decide to
use regarding my WWII history, feel assured that I'm comfortable
with your good judgment.

Sincerely,

Drith
Arthur B. Schultz

PS: William James writes ". . . What we need to discover in
the social realm is the moral equivalent of war: something heroic
that will speak to men as universally as war does, and yet will
be compatible with their spiritual selves as war has proved
itself to be incompatible. "The Varieties of Religious
Experience" 1902.

FOREWORD

Arthur "Dutch" Schultz, Carol Schultz Vento's father, was a genuine war hero, much decorated, much revered, a paratrooper in the storied 82nd Airborne Division who jumped into Normandy on D-Day, fought in the snows of Belgium at the Battle of the Bulge and endured countless battlefield encounters with the brutality and senseless tragedy of war. Once at home, his experiences were memorialized in American culture through Daryl F. Zanuck's 1960 film *The Longest Day* and the works of Steven Ambrose. He was everything we wanted all our warriors to be—brave, modest, and steadfast in the face of danger. But there was, as his daughter Carol Schultz Vento so movingly recounts in *Hidden Legacy*, another Dutch Schultz, another reality, one that the public did not see. Like millions of other veterans, Dutch Schultz returned home, haunted by his wartime experiences; he struggled with alcoholism; his family life disintegrated; he married three times, and, even late in his life, after a successful career in the drug and alcohol addiction field, he still struggled with war trauma. His was an untold story—but it was not an unusual one.

Sixteen million men and women served in the American armed forces during the Second World War, and their powerful battlefield experiences at Iwo Jima, Normandy, or Salerno have been told and retold, recorded in oral histories, and inscribed in film, fiction, and historical accounts, but what took place when these millions of G.I.s returned home at war's end has been a long-neglected story. Unlike the tortured veterans of Vietnam or the forgotten veterans of Korea, whose readjustment problems have received considerable public analysis, we are repeatedly told that the veterans of the Second World War did not face such problems. They had fought "the good war," triumphed, and returned home to a grateful nation, happy, healthy, and well-adjusted. However, this comfortable assumption that "the boys" returned home psychically and emotionally unscathed, that no one drank too much or abused his wife or children, could not be further from the truth. Roughly 1.3 million American service personnel received some kind of psychological wound during World War II. Although many veterans returned to civilian life with little apparent difficulty, for some, the war and its trauma could not be left behind. In 1945, ten thousand veterans every month were reporting what medical authorities described as some form "of psychoneurotic disorder," and those numbers continued to rise in 1946 and 1947. In that latter year, over half the beds in VA hospitals were occupied by men suffering from "psychoneurotic" symptoms. Post-traumatic stress syndrome did not have a name until 1980, but in the aftermath of the Second World War, depression, recurring nightmares, survivor guilt, outbursts of rage, most frequently directed at family members, "exaggerated startle responses," and anxiety reactions—all of which are recognized today as classic symptoms of post-traumatic stress disorder—were as common as they were unnerving.

For many, the nightmares and other symptoms set in immediately and lingered for decades; for others, the problems did not begin until long after combat, when memories of the war, they believed, had been long buried. Since no one wanted to have NP (Neuropsychiatric) stamped on his records, there is every reason to believe—just as there is with today's veterans—that those numbers represent only the tip of the iceberg. It wasn't a good idea to admit to having war-related psychological problems. Despite the blizzard of magazine articles and books attempting to educate the public about these psychoneurotic symptoms, prejudice was still powerful.

And as Carol Schultz Vento's story makes achingly clear, it was not only the veteran who suffered but his family as well. Dr. William C. Menninger, chief psychiatric consultant to the surgeon general of the Army, came to believe that soldiers' wives were the "forgotten" casualties of the war. "Nobody gave them any glamour, and few gave them much support. Along with their soldiers, they had to 'sweat it out' in insecurity and uncertainty. They tried to live from day to day, just waiting." Then, for many, there was the unexpectedly difficult homecoming. "My mother told beautiful stories of their courtship before the war," one Wisconsin woman wrote about her parents, "but he was a different man when he returned." He landed at Normandy, losing friends there and in the subsequent fighting. When he came home, "my parents fought constantly; my father drank constantly. He was seldom happy . . . Everyone who knew my father before the war said he was never the same."

In the end, children bore many of their father's scars. Born just after the war, a New Jersey man told me that he grew up "tiptoeing around" his veteran father, who suffered from terrible nightmares and a serious drinking problem. His father watched the old 1950s films on TV, films in which the war was presented as "noble and just and heroic," and would then "cry for hours, a drink constantly by his side." One woman's father, who had spent much of the war in a Japanese prison camp, returned with an undiagnosed and untreated PTSD that kept her "family from living full and normal lives, lives others take for granted . . . I was never 'Daddy's little girl,'" she laments, "but I certainly was his POW."

These problems undoubtedly contributed to another often overlooked aspect of the war's aftermath. Americans did marry in record numbers during the war, but they also divorced in record numbers when it ended. Between 1945 and 1947, petitions for divorce flooded the courts, and, as the V.A. duly reported, the divorce rate for veterans was twice as high as for civilians. The United States experienced what newspapers and magazines referred to as a "divorce boom." Stories of breakups and bigamy, adultery and marital strife filled the papers. In 1946, the United States recorded the highest divorce rate in the world—and American history. It was a figure not to be equaled until 1973.

Even with the ongoing interest in the Second World War, there is hardly a whisper about these troubling experiences, as if to raise unpleasant realities is somehow to tarnish the image of the "Greatest Generation." It does not. Hence, the great importance of Carol Schultz Vento's courageously honest account of her family's travails, of her hero father's struggle with the aftershocks of war, and the lifelong impact that that struggle had on his family. Her story is a daughter's personal account. It is moving, at times heartbreaking, but it is also much more. It is a call to remember the lasting impact of war, however just or necessary, on those who fight it and those who love them. Carol Schultz Vento's testimonial, and others like it, does not diminish the wartime generation's accomplishments, but rather it suggests that the price they paid was far higher, the toll extracted from them and their families far greater, and their struggles far more protracted than the glossy tributes to the "Greatest Generation" would have us believe. It is, in the end, a cautionary tale, reminding us that if we send soldiers into harm's way, we should be under no illusions about war's colossal human costs, remembering that even in the most brilliant triumphs, there is heartbreak and that the suffering does not stop when the shooting does.

—Thomas Childers, Author of
*Soldier From the War Returning:
The Greatest Generation's Troubled
Homecoming from World War II*

FOREWORD

Arthur "Dutch" Schultz. Stephen Ambrose gave me his name as I was looking for WWII Veterans to interview for the documentary I was directing on the making of Steven Spielberg's film *Saving Private Ryan*. After one conversation with Dutch, I knew that he was no ordinary man, and I wanted to do something special for him. On the day we began filming, I purposely scheduled Dutch's interview directly before Mr. Spielberg's. I worked it out so that Dutch would finish just as Steven arrived. Just as I had hoped, they met and immediately connected. Steven shut down the shoot for nearly an hour as Dutch captivated him with stories of parachuting into Normandy on D-Day and fighting at the Battle of the Bulge.

Steven was gracious and genuinely interested in Dutch's every word. Dutch was modest and appreciative of how his dramatic accounts were being celebrated as great acts of bravery. But when Dutch spoke about the war, it wasn't with a glossy filter. He said it plain and simple; "War is Hell," and candidly added that for him, returning home with those horrific memories was even worse. The terror wreaked havoc on his life and his family in a way that never really ended. It was only buried.

I stayed in touch with Dutch until he passed away. He was wise and kind and encouraged me to "believe in myself." We frequently spoke on the phone and visited in person when we could. Long before I met his daughter, Carol Schultz Vento, I heard *all* about her from her Dad. Every time I talked to Dutch, he would say, "You know, my daughter's a lawyer with a Ph.D." He called her "remarkable" and "incredibly smart." That is an understatement.

Carol's candid accounts of what it was like growing up in the dark shadow of a war-torn father are emotional and riveting. Dutch had so many of the wonderful qualities talked about in the "Greatest Generation," but as he would be the first to tell you, it took more than a few

THE HIDDEN LEGACY OF WORLD WAR II

generations for him to harness the demons that followed him home from war. Like many of the WWII veterans that I interviewed, Dutch held the horror inside for decades, and the repercussions were devastating to the people who loved him. In a letter Dutch wrote me after the interview, he said that before I questioned him about the war, he had "no memory of some of the incidents that I talked about." It's frightening to imagine what could be so terrifying that your mind would not allow you to remember.

As you will see in the intimate details of *The Hidden Legacy of World War II*, it was a painful and inspiring journey for everyone involved. Arthur "Dutch" Schultz was a hero on the battlefield who spent a lifetime fighting the relentless anguish of war. His amazing daughter, Carol Schultz Vento, embraced another kind of bravery. She was brave enough to recount the trauma it created in her own life and, even more courageous, wrote this captivating book about it. I know Dutch would be so proud.

—Christen Harty Schaefer, Writer/Producer
of *Saving Private Ryan: Into the Breach*

Introduction

THE OTHER SIDE OF THE "GOOD WAR"

*The war was fun for America. I'm not talking about the poor souls
who lost sons and daughters. But to the rest of us, the war was a hell
of a good time.*

—Quoted in Studs Terkel, *The Good War:
An Oral History of World War II"*

Children, fathers and war—three words that are not typically linked.
This book is a daughter's exploration of the untold story of the human
drama that World War II brought into the family.

When World War II ended on September 2, 1945, millions of battle-
weary men began the long trek home, hoping to return to normalcy.
Marriages were numerous and often hasty; the highest rate ever recorded—16.4 marriages per 1000 people—occurred in 1946.[1] According to
the Census Bureau, 75.8 million children were born in the postwar years
of 1946 to 1964, with males slightly exceeding females. Many of these
Baby Boomers were born to the 16.2 million World War II veterans,
children who, for the most part, have remained silent about Dad's war.

Popular culture has mythologized World War II as the "Good War,"
a phrase coined by Studs Terkel in the title of his 1984 book. In *The
Best War Ever—America and World War II,* a noted historian, Michael
C. C. Adams, stated that Americans have viewed World War II and its
aftermath as a "golden age" and an "idyllic period."[2] However, it wasn't
until the 1990s, a half-century after the end of the war, that Tom Brokaw
and Stephen Ambrose institutionalized the myth. Tom Brokaw, in *The
Greatest Generation*, portrayed the World War II vet as being the greatest
generation any society has ever produced. In his paean to World War

1. "U.S. fertility at low and life expectancy at high," *New York Times,* September 8, 1987.
2. Michael C.C. Adams, *The Best War Ever—America and World War II* (Baltimore: The Johns Hopkins
University Press, 1994), xiii.

II, *Citizen Soldiers*, Steven Ambrose described, in an extremely readable fashion, not only the personalities of the men but also their experience in battle and how it formed them into the men who "built modern America . . . The 'we' generation of World War II was a special breed of men . . . who did great things for America and the world."[3]

It took a Baby Boomer, however, to bring the vivid, horrific reality of our fathers' war to his generation. Steven Spielberg, in *Saving Private Ryan*, gave the boomers and their children a visual immersion into the blood and gore of World War II. For many of the war veterans' progeny, that was the "aha" moment. Spielberg, the son of a World War II veteran of the Burma campaign, had heard and absorbed his father's war stories. Spielberg said that as he grew older, he "began to resent the misconception among Americans that Vietnam was the most painful war, simply because we saw it regularly in color and on TV . . . I never felt the World War II veteran had his story told the way it happened to them."[4]

A few years after the release of *Private Ryan*, a crack appeared in the wall of silence; reality collided with the myth of the good war. Books by offspring of World War II vets began to appear. Books, such as Julia Collins' *My Father's War* and Tom Mathews' *Our Fathers' War: Growing Up in the Shadow of the Greatest Generation*, drew the curtain back and described their troubled postwar home lives. It is indisputable that World War II fathers had their lives altered by military service. Some of these changes were positive and helped to fuel the good war narrative. The Servicemen's Readjustment Act of 1944, commonly known as the GI bill, gave millions an opportunity for a college education. By 1947, veterans constituted half of "enrolled college students," and the tidal wave of war veteran college graduates began.[5] The lasting impact of the GI Bill was to transform America into a middle-class nation.[6] But for some families, the war never ended. Unrecognized war trauma contributed to fathers' struggles and exposed some of their children to major life challenges like

---

3. Stephen E. Ambrose, *Citizen Soldier: The U.S. Army From the Normandy Beaches to the Bulge to the Surrender of Germany* (New York: Simon and Schuster, 1997), 472.

4. "Steven Spielberg and Tom Hanks," *Rochester Democrat and Chronicle*, July 24, 1998.

5. Suzanne Mettler, *Soldiers to Citizens—The GI Bill and the Making of the Greatest Generation* (New York: Oxford University Press, 2005), 67.

6. Michael J. Bennett, *When Dreams Came True—The GI Bill and the Making of Modern America* (Washington: Brassey's, 1996), 315.

divorce, alcoholism, and suicide. Other children, whose fathers remained in the home and functioned well as the family's provider, never understood the reasons for their fathers' rage, aloofness, or detachment.

Prior to this, very little had been studied or written regarding the negative impact of World War II on the combatants. Even though "it would be difficult to find any war in which participants did not claim that the actualities of combat had in some way altered their character," that was somehow left out of our national narrative about the "good war." However, a "deep and profound alteration of identity had taken place."[7] Combat had changed our fathers, but there was little documentation, in academic studies or media reports, about the psychological aftershock of their battles.

Dr. Matthew Friedman, Executive Director of the National Center for Post-Traumatic Stress Disorder, noted that there were not any large-scale studies on combat stress and World War II veterans. PTSD was not a diagnosis in the Diagnostic and Statistical Manual (DSM) until 1980 after the Vietnam War had ended, and a constellation of symptoms was observed in the returning veterans of that war and recognized as war trauma. Previously, the mental health label placed on war veterans from World War II and Korea by the Veterans Administration was typically anxiety neurosis.[8] A therapist for the Veterans Administration and an academic who has dealt with Vietnam-era combat-induced mental health issues, Dr. Raymond Scurfield noted that there are more similarities than differences in our modern-era wars. A universality of all wars that Dr. Scurfield has recognized is the burden placed on the individual warrior after homecoming to deal with their own anguish.[9] The myth of the well-adjusted World War II veteran left little room for the reality that the war "was a horrible experience," which left lasting scars on the combat-exposed veterans and, in some cases, on their families.[10]

The heavy burdens on the returning World War II veterans were not widely acknowledged. Some research on veterans diagnosed with combat exhaustion, traumatic war neurosis, or operational fatigue was done in the early years after the war, but those studies were limited, with small

7. Eric J. Leed, *No Man's Land* (New York: Cambridge University Press, 1979), 1.
8. Matthew Friedman, Ph.D., M.D., phone interview by author, May 24, 2007.
9. Raymond Scurfield, Ph.D., email interview by author, March 19, 2007.
10. Adams, *The Best War Ever*, xiv.

sample sizes. Often, the focus was on prisoners of war and World War II veterans with symptoms severe enough that they sought help from the Veteran's Administration.[11]

The lack of support for the physically and mentally traumatized World War II veteran and the creation of the good war myth most likely occurred because only a minority of men were exposed to combat situations. Figures vary as to the number of men who actually saw combat, but one estimate states that only twenty-five percent of the army was assigned to ground combat divisions.[12] According to Gerald Linderman, "fewer than one million, probably no more than 800,000, saw extended combat."[13] A little-known fact is that twenty-five percent of the over sixteen million in the military during the war never even left the United States.[14]

The perception that all fought equally in World War II is false. All who served contributed mightily to the war effort, and their roles were important. However, the young men who experienced combat situations were the exception to the norm. Combat exposure also varied among the divisions in the military. In the Army and Marine Corps, the infantry, combat engineer, tank, airborne, artillery units, medics, and bomber and fighter pilots had high rates of battle fatigue. However, Navy and Coast Guard rates were lower, the exception being those crews subjected to kamikaze attacks and ship sinkings.[15] In any case, neither combat exposure nor post-traumatic stress disorder has been adequately measured. As my father said, "After the war, no one wanted to hear what combat was really like." The heavy burden of combat took a toll on many of those men who carried the weight of battle on their shoulders. War causes a change in everyone, and many World War II veterans were able to manage the changes and function well, but some did not. By focusing on those from World War II who struggled more with their demons of war, I hope to shine a spotlight on this forgotten group and attempt to understand the sacrifices that they made in all of our names.

---

11. Paula Schnurr, "PTSD and Combat-Related Psychiatric Symptoms in Older Veterans," *PTSD Research Quarterly* 2 (1) (Winter 1991), 1–6.

12. John C. McManus, *The American Combat Soldier in World War II* (Novato, CA: Presidio, 1988), 3.

13. Gerard Linderman, *The World Within War: America's Combat Experience in World War II* (New York: The Free Press, 1997), 1.

14. Adams, *The Best War Ever*, 70.

15. Brian Chermol, "Wounds without Scars: Treatment of Battle Fatigue in the U.S. Armed Forces in the Second World War," *Military Affairs* 49, no. 1 (January 1985), 10.

Some of the World War II veterans, who functioned well for most of their lives, find that their war memories become overwhelming in old age. In recent years, analyzing the emergence of physical and psychological problems in these veterans later in life has slowly become a topic of interest to researchers. Studies that have compared veterans with non-veterans show higher rates of alcoholism, heart disease, dementia, and delayed post-traumatic stress disorder in combat-exposed veterans.[16] With these recent findings, it is clear that war has a lifelong impact on the combatant and, therefore, his family.

The impact on a child of having a combat veteran father from the World War II era has not been a topic of interest, even though it has been found that combat veterans' first marriages were much more likely to end in divorce.[17] A solitary study from 1986, done by Robert Rosenheck, looked at a sample of five families and found, not surprisingly to those of us who lived through the experience, that the offspring of World War II fathers with PTSD suffered from trans-generational effects.[18] Most of the studies done in the twentieth century regarding the impact on children with a father with PTSD are from the Vietnam War era.

The children of World War II have been relatively silent about what went on behind closed doors. Some families were fairly well-adjusted, and their fathers were able to repress or control the impact of the horrors of war. Those whose fathers couldn't escape the haunting memories dealt with severe family dysfunction, and the children felt isolated, not connecting their father's difficulties to the war.

The narrative history presented in my book gives an insight into the impact of the war filtered through a daughter's lens. My paratrooper Dad's fighting spirit and bravery influenced me in my childhood and helped form me into the type of woman I became. The Baby Boomer tradition of pushing the limits could be a result of having World War II Dads as role models. Resilience and capability are a constant theme found in most stories of World War II. However, the positive effects of

16. "Male Combat Veterans Rank High in Heart Disease Risk," *Science Daily*, May 4, 2005, available from http://sciencedaily.com/releases/2005/05/050504003733.htm; "Traumatic Stress Disorder, Dementia Linked in WWII Vets," *Science Daily*, January 14, 2000, available from http://sciencedaily.com/releases/2000/01/000113233143.htm.

17. "Combat Vets Much More Likely to Divorce, Separate," *Mental Health Resources*, December 20, 2002, available from http://mentalhealth.about.com/library/sci/1202blvet1202.htm.

18. Robert Rosenheck, "Impact of Posttraumatic Stress Disorder of World War II on the Next Generation," *Journal of Nervous and Mental Disorders*, 174 (6) (June 1986), 319–27.

the war are counterbalanced by the reality of living with the combatant Dad, who never truly left the battleground. It is these stories that need to be told if we are to lift the veil that has obscured the other legacy of the Greatest Generation.

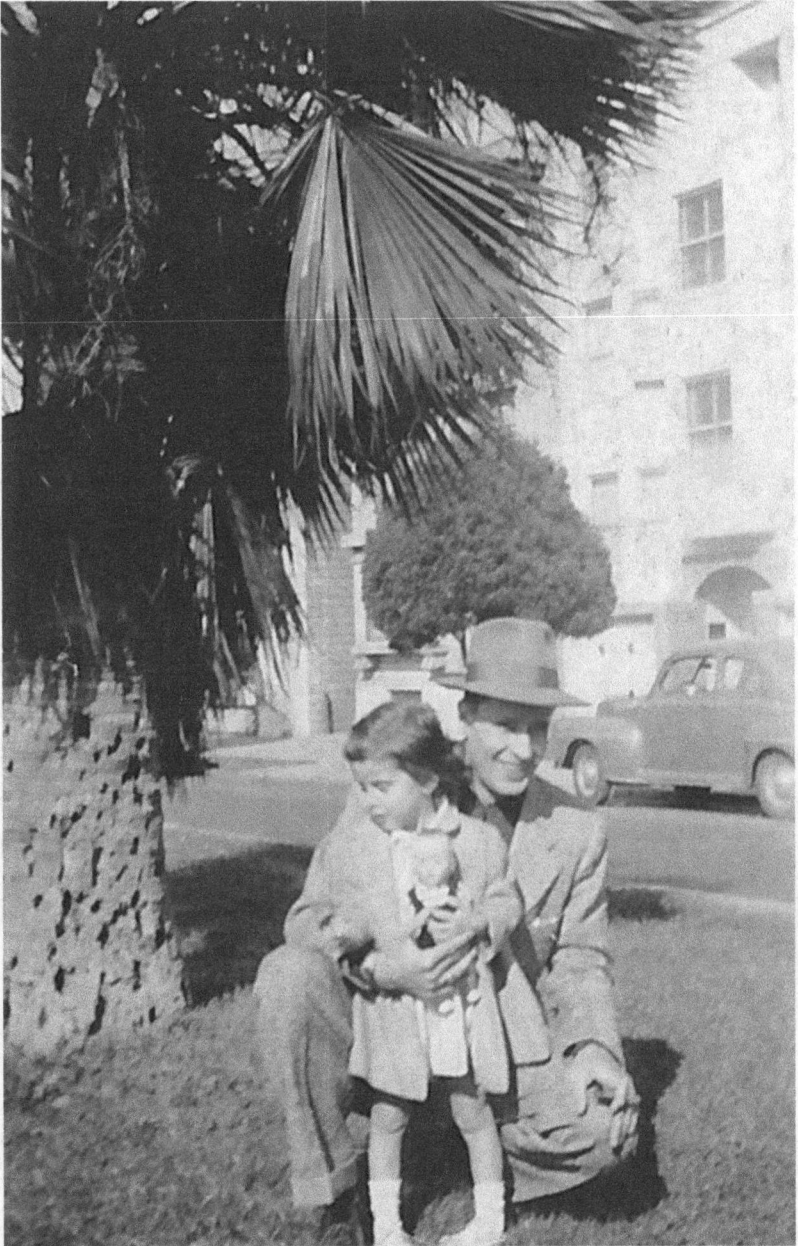

Carol and father "Dutch" in San Francisco in the late 1940's.

Carol & Dutch - first communion.

1

DESERT WARFARE

Skeet Shooting

Clouds hid earth from sky, invisible as you
strapped in a chute, hanging in the Normandy night

Until tracer flares, machine guns split the dark
a clay pigeon had more chance of staying whole.

I listen for the thud of your chute,
collapsing, slapping the ground,

for the thump of your feet, planting
in sodden pastures, boxed in by hedgerows

where German snipers hid. There you stayed
rooted in fear, though you went on fighting,

drinking, fathering, piecing together shards
into a replica that shattered each time

a car backfired, or a baby wailed.
Your footsteps filled with muddy water.

I fit my sneakers in their shape.
I walk breathing your fear.

I cut a willow branch and trace your name
scrawled across the sky as you fell.

—Emily Warn, *Voices in Wartime Anthology*,
reprinted with permission of the author,
daughter of a World War II paratrooper

Tacos and transmissions. Dirty brown air trapped in the soup bowl of San Bernardino. A rose-colored angular building jutting out at the corner of Sagebrush and Willow projected an image of false cheer inside. Just like the town, the rehab hospital had an aura of gloom. Surly nurses, their numbers tempered by the occasional young aide with a genuine smile, mumbled terse responses to our questions, directing us to a barren room in the farthest corner of the structure.

The odor tipped me off even before I entered. A sickly, sweet freshener impotently attempted to liven up the stale air. The old man lay on his side in the soiled hospital bed, semi-fetal position, with one khaki-covered leg hanging to the floor. Anxiously circling the bed to get a view, I saw a stubbled, sunken face, slightly reminiscent of a death mask. The brownish, grey hair was jutting out cowlick mad. The nails were so long they almost curled. I touched the man's shoulder, and a gnarled, discolored hand grabbed my wrist. "I haven't felt this bad since the Bulge." The Battle of the Bulge, sixty years prior, was his reference point for death.

I had traveled 3,000 miles to rescue Arthur 'Dutch' Schultz, the war hero. World War II, the defining point of his life, had brought him recognition and praise, but at the same time, it had also haunted him, contributing to postwar tragedy and loss.

My mission was not strange to me. In some ways, I had been rescuing my Dad ever since my post-war birth, ten months after he had returned from the European Theater. My lifetime obligation had been to ensure Dad's emotional survival. This final foray also focused on physical release. Get Dad out of the rehab center and back home so that he could die surrounded by his medals and his dog. He had been left, sixty miles from home, at the desert facility while his third wife, a retired TWA stewardess, went to a fund raising gala in Chicago. I was a continent away and becoming increasingly more panicked by the day. Dad had developed pneumonia, a serious condition for an aged man with emphysema and congestive heart failure, and because of the inadequacy of care at the center, he had also fallen and lacerated his head when his repeated calls for help on getting to the bathroom had gone unheeded. I was making multiple phone calls to the nursing station daily. Dad was increasingly anxious, his once booming voice weakening and quivering as he asked me repeatedly to take him home. Orders were clear. My master sergeant had directed me to get him "out of this place."

Dad had taken me along on his journey, and now, at the end of the road, at his bedside, I was trying to make sense of my feelings. A mixture of pride, pity, and anger roiled inside me, like pea soup just ready to boil. Tamping down my emotions, I projected steely resolve, the stoic child that Dad had trained.

Wife number three entered the room, having just returned from her vacation. With platinum hair and fire engine red acrylic nails, she appeared decades younger than the emaciated figure in the bed, instead of the mere sixteen years that separated them. Dad's long, bony finger pointed accusingly toward her as he barked, "It's your fault that I'm here!" Their relationship had begun thirty-some years earlier and was now bitter and contentious, even though it had had such a promising beginning and had been relatively peaceful for a number of years. When attention in the nineteen-nineties turned to the World II veterans who were belatedly dubbed the "Greatest Generation," Dad's wife had basked in the reflected glow of the war hero's spouse, enjoying the company of such notables as Stephen Ambrose and Steven Spielberg, who featured Dad in books and documentaries. However, as my father's emphysema and COPD worsened in the late nineties, so did the state of his last marriage. Arguments between the two became the norm. My father became increasingly isolated from family members and close friends throughout these later years, and as Dad weakened physically and emotionally, my sense of responsibility for him grew.

I had a feeling that the journey west in October 2005 would be my last trip to visit Dad. I was accompanied by my close friend Ilene, and it was she who convinced his wife that he would get better care at an acute care hospital closer to their home. Two muscular young men coddled my 110 lb. skeletal father and strapped him tightly onto a gurney for transport. With oxygen tubing in his nose, IVs in his arm, and a raspy voice, he told war stories, giving especially vivid descriptions of his harrowing D-Day jump before being packed into the ambulance.

As we followed northward, he waved to us, relieved at his temporary escape. In the hometown hospital with his doctor, he seemed to rally a bit, a ruddy color slowly suffusing his gray cheeks. After a few days, I left him to return back East. The farewell was wrenching. As I leaned over to hug him goodbye, he murmured, "My baby girl, my baby girl," in a choked voice over and over, then ordered me out of his room so that I wouldn't see the old guy cry.

Two weeks later, he was dead. I had succeeded in carrying out Dad's last orders. Immobile at home for only two days, with his dog and mementos of his war glory—medals, citations, miniature parachutes—surrounding him, Dad finally joined the war dead for whom he had always mourned. His salvation at the Bulge was providential, but for all his bravado and success, Dad had returned home from the war a shattered and broken man.

The next time I saw my father, he was delivered to me in a box. Receiving the remnants of my father's cremated body on Halloween seemed oddly appropriate. Answering the door, I expected the cry of "Trick or Treat" from neighborhood kids, but instead, the UPS driver handed me a worn cardboard box with the return address of Victor Valley Mortuary, Victorville, CA. His wife had directed the mortician to deliver Dad's ashes to me since there was not to be a memorial service in California. Before his death, Dad and I, with approval from his wife, had agreed he would be buried at Arlington National Cemetery. Untying the dirty white strings wrapped around the box, I tore off the shopping bag paper and pulled out the remains of my father. A shiny gold urn shaped like a square held the former strong and dynamic paratrooper. For the next six weeks, Dad looked over my living room from my mantle—the longest period my father and I had lived in a house together since my parent's divorce when I was eleven. I carried him with me for the final time on December 7, 2005, for his interment in Arlington. The night prior to the ceremony, Dad left my arms forever. I handed him over to his wife at the door of her hotel room, and she placed the gleaming container on the cherry wood bureau. A brisk winter wind chilled me the next morning. As I said my last goodbye to my father at the grave site, I was a part of the group of mourners but alone with my memories.

"Hut—two—three—four. Hut—two—three—four." The cadence of my childhood. Echoing footsteps on worn, wooden floors. Memories of a spindly, pale child with purplish under-eye circles marching behind her athletic paratrooper Dad. Up and down the narrow Philadelphia row house steps, past the shoebox-sized bedrooms, the stark no-sink bathroom, and the musty coal bin, the six-year-old girl's mission was to not give up, just like Dad. In 1952, my father was in his late twenties and had the physique of the welterweight boxer and baseball player that he once was. Tall, with mercurial blue-green eyes and light brown hair, Dad had a rakish smile that charmed every woman he met. I didn't know it at the time, but my father had been the boxing champion of his 82nd Airborne regiment and a combat survivor of the European Campaign in World War II, including the bloody and confused D-Day and the nightmarish Battle of the Bulge. To me, he was just Daddy—and my hero. In appearance, we could have been a study in contrasts, the All-American young man with his little Italian waif of a daughter. I inherited my mother's dark-eyed Mediterranean looks, but in temperament and interests, I mirrored Dad. Our marching game was all I knew of my father's war during my childhood. Dad was silent about his negative war experiences, and my youthful view of his war was blurred by the representations of D-Day on the big screen, so it wasn't until later on in life that I realized that his war wasn't all fun and games. The traumas that he experienced during his combat years haunted him for decades and had a huge impact on my family.

Dutch Schultz's Normandy war was portrayed in the 1962 World War epic movie, *The Longest Day*, based on the bestselling book about D-Day by Cornelius Ryan. The glossy film program, distributed at the ornate center city Philadelphia premiere, anointed my father as the citizen soldier symbolic of the 73,000 Americans who participated in D-Day. I sat in the audience as he stood handsomely and expensively suited on stage at the glitzy showing that year. The audience cheered lustily for him, but I was a petulant fifteen-year-old that evening. While my father was feted and made to be the center of attention, my sister and I were relegated to the last row of the theater, along with my sister's godfather, Dad's World War II buddy and fellow paratrooper, Joe Tallett. I felt fancy in my red and white flocked dress, Rosemary was poufed out in blue taffeta, and Dad was with the dignitaries in the front, next to his fashionable blonde girlfriend. My irritation arose not so much from our "peanut gallery" seating but my crushing disappointment with the evening. Dad didn't introduce me to Paul Anka, one of the young stars of the movie and an early sixties teenage singing heartthrob, whose eight by ten glossies were plastered on my bedroom wall. That night not only fueled my adolescent pique, the movie influenced my perception of Dad's war for decades.

The Longest Day depicted Dutch Schultz as an eager, confused, and sometimes clueless 82nd Airborne paratrooper who landed behind enemy lines far from his drop zone. Well-portrayed by a hyperactive Richard Beymer, in a memorable scene, Dutch won twenty-five hundred dollars in gambling winnings the night before D-Day. Right then, a letter from his mother arrived containing rosary beads, which fueled his fear of certain death if he pocketed the illicit gains. Further scenes show Dutch hanging in a tree, his parachute stuck. After freeing himself, he then wandered far from his drop zone. However, all seemed to end well, with my father eventually rejoining troopers from the 101st Airborne. The final movie moments find the young trooper sitting and smoking cigarettes with a wounded RAF pilot, played by Richard Burton. The flier aptly summed up D-Day with a classic line from the movie—"I'm hurt, he's dead, and you're lost"—dead referring to the German soldier lying nearby with his boots on the wrong feet. To me, Dad's war did not seem so bad; it was in black and white, not very bloody. He seemed pretty relaxed at the end of that fateful day.

Dutch at Anaheim Angels stadium with manager Mike Scioscia (right), June 6, 2004.

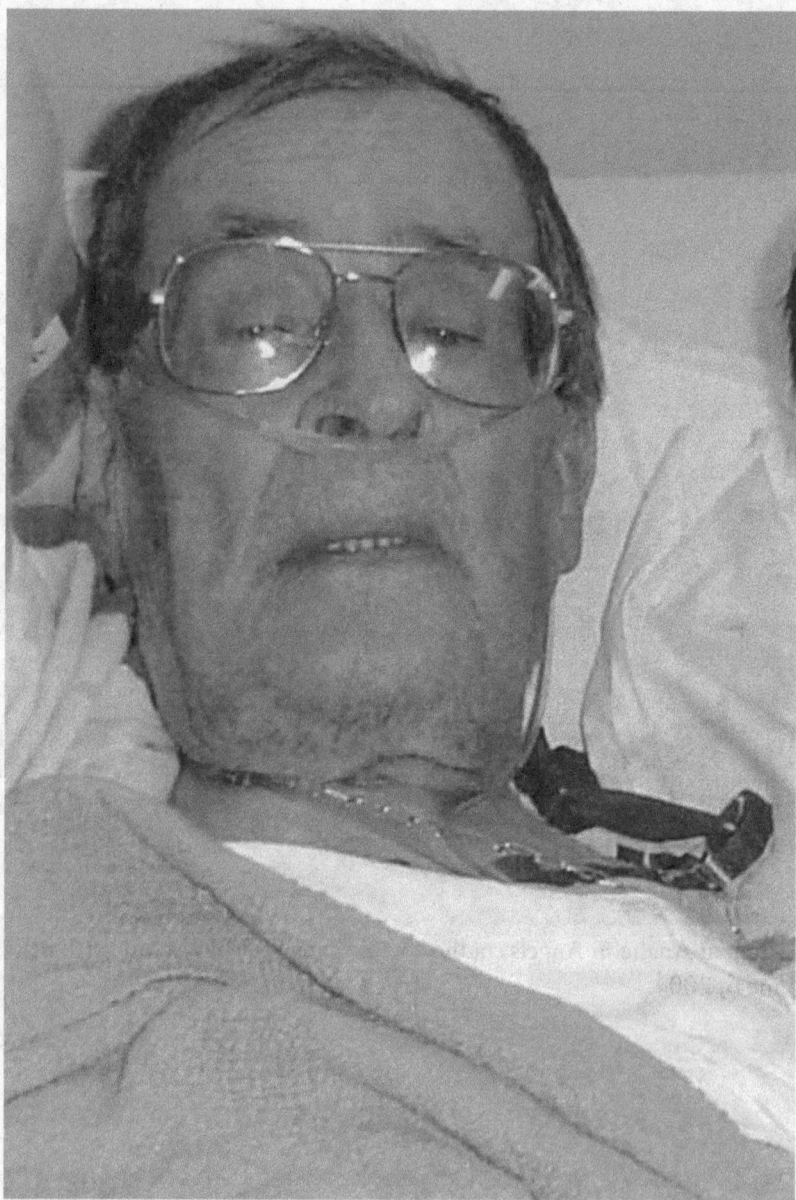

Dutch in October, 2005.

2

ALL AMERICAN

Franklin Spencer . . . who was forced to abandon a wounded GI on the morning of D-Day, is still haunted by the vision of that man nearly sixty years later. In an interview, Spencer said that no movie or book could ever fully portray the horror of combat: the smell of rotting flesh and splattered blood are with him more than half a century later. "There isn't any glamour to it," he said of war. "It's just something terrible that happens to young people who had nothing to do with causing it. No winners, all losers. Anybody who glorifies it is crazy."

—Quoted in *Combat Jump*, Ed Ruggero, 2003

Emotional angst accompanied my rational exploration of Dad's war. Proud of his accomplishments but angry at the silence surrounding the destruction of our family, I walled off my feelings by delving into academic research of the 82nd Airborne history during World War II. I had seen my father portrayed in movies, interviewed in World War II documentaries, and read about him in books, but I never probed him about what I had seen or read. It wasn't until my midlife foray into therapy that I understood how much my father's war had shaped the type of woman that I had become. My therapist, the son of a World War II combat veteran, was a valuable aid in connecting war trauma to my generation. Two years before Dad died in 2005, I finally asked my father the tough questions, and he answered them, grateful and maybe a bit relieved to finally share some of his turmoil with me. That day, I cobbled together an incomplete narrative, once removed, of Dad's war.

"Buddy, you got a smoke?" Dutch said to the first dead man he saw. On June 6, 1944, the young paratrooper had been wandering through the hedgerows of Normandy for hours. Shadows and mortar booms were his only companions. He tripped over a pair of boots, sticking awkwardly out of the bushes. Relieved to make contact and hoping to get a cigarette, he reached over to nudge the sleeping soldier and saw the perfectly round bullet hole in the middle of his forehead.[1]

Just three hours earlier, a terrified Dutch had been on a bouncing C-47 with a mortar squad of paratroopers, flak bouncing off the fuselage. As he clutched his mother's rosary beads, the plane went into a precipitous dive. Frantically, the stick rushed out into a sky full of enemy fire, jumping at 250 feet, far too low. The plane crashed, and a fireball exploded as Dutch slammed into the earth with a bang, wrenching his back.

Lost and scared, Dutch had to find his drop zone and the rest of his regiment. The 82nd Airborne's goal on D-Day was to capture the town of Sainte Mere Eglise behind enemy lines. A successful mission would disrupt the German military movement toward Utah Beach. Utah, Omaha, Juno, and Gold were the Allied code names for the French beaches targeted for a monumental Allied amphibious assault. Allied occupation of Sainte Mere Eglise was crucial in order to avoid a Utah Beach massacre. In addition to the dangerous prospect of facing the tough units of Germany's Seventh Army, major problems had plagued the drop of the 505th regiment, along with the other units of the 82nd heading towards the town and the important bridge of La Fiere.[2] Hundreds had already been killed, wounded, or lost. After many hours alone, Dutch finally found some troopers. According to the movie *The Longest Day*, Dutch Schultz met up with a group from the 101st Airborne and missed all the D-Day action.

The reality, however, was somewhat different. Dutch was first found by his platoon leader, Jack Tallerday, who had gathered up other stray troopers from the 101st and the 82nd's 507th and 508th. Lieutenant Tallerday left the group huddled by a hedgerow while he went searching for the drop zone. An hour passed, and Tallerday did not return. Therefore, Dutch and the others decided to walk down the road, single file, towards the sound of mortars. Dead and wounded troopers littered the

---

1. Cornelius Ryan, "Schultz, PFC Arthur B. "Dutch" interview, May 8, 1958, "The Longest Day," Cornelius Ryan Collection of World War II Papers, Box 8, Folder 40, Archives and Special Collections, Ohio University Libraries, Athens, Ohio, 3.

2. David Howarth, *The Sixth of June 1944* (New York: McGraw Hill, 1959), 86.

side of the road, and one of those paratroopers lying alongside the road was Lieutenant Jack Tallerday. Dutch thought Tallerday was dead.

> Dutch: I didn't bother to go check him because there was no movement. He was totally white. I couldn't believe what was happening. I made no effort to go over to him. I was convinced he was dead . . . what had happened is he had been hit, and the original medic and several others that followed overloaded him with morphine. He had all appearances of being dead.

As the wandering group of about thirty men approached more and more violence, they ducked into an apple orchard to avoid shelling. Suddenly, the Germans discovered the troopers and pounded them with mortars, scattering them in all directions. Chaos and confusion reigned among the inexperienced soldiers. There was a complete lack of organization—no officers or NCOs were around. Earlier on D-Day, the 505's Battalion Commander, Major Kellam, and the Executive Officer, Major McGinty, had been killed. Captain Stefanich, C company Commander was seriously wounded. All of Dutch's platoon and assistant platoon leaders had been wounded.

Dutch and the others in the small group were in combat for the first time. It wasn't until late afternoon on D-Day that the youthful, inexperienced soldiers received any direction.[3] The 505's regimental commander, General James Gavin, gathered up about one hundred wandering men, including my father, from various units of the 82nd and 101st divisions. In the late hours of June 6th they headed to Ste. Mere Eglise. Gavin assigned the men to locations along the railroad tracks not far from the La Fiere Bridge. They dug themselves foxholes for the night, artillery shells raining down all night long.[4]

> Dutch: I heard this horrendous screaming and screaming and screaming . . . It seemed like it lasted eternally . . . I don't know who it was who was hit. I know that I was alone by then. I was

3. Stephen Ambrose, "Schultz," Kalikow Collection, National WWII Museum, New Orleans, LA, 9.
4. James Gavin, *On to Berlin: Battles of an Airborne Commander 1943–1946* (New York: Viking Press, 1978), 106–109.

in a hole next to somebody, but I didn't know him. I'm not sure I got any sleep that night.[5]

Dawn broke on June 7th, and the battle at La Fiere Bridge raged on. La Fiere was a crucial target, and the fighting was brutal and gruesome. For days, control of the five-hundred-yard causeway flipped between Americans and Germans, and Dutch was in the thick of it. The sounds and smells of death and suffering surrounded him. A close buddy was struck by a mortar—half his face was blown off, but he was still alive. A paratrooper BAR man placed his gun against the wounded soldier's forehead and pulled the trigger. Dutch had witnessed a mercy killing on the battlefield.

> Dutch: this baptism of fire was beyond all expectations I had
> about what war was like. It was a horrible experience. I'm ever so
> grateful that I had the experience. I feel that I served with some
> of the bravest and most courageous men of WWII . . . I stayed
> with the 82nd until the end of the war. But I shall never, never
> experience the kind of fear that I experienced that day on 6th
> June 1944 because I don't remember much else than the fear.[6]

Four days later, American troopers finally prevailed, with the bulk of the struggle on the final day falling to G Company, 325th Glider Infantry Regiment, along with the 507th. The 82nd had taken heavy casualties from days of unrelenting combat, with men continuing to battle with little sleep and minimal food. Because of the 505's and the other units of the 82nd's ultimate victory at La Fiere Bridge, German troops were critically delayed. The paratroopers of the 82nd had cleared the way for the advance of Maj. Gen. J. Lawton Collins' VII Corps, which was coming from Utah Beach. The Nazis were unable to inflict carnage on the soldiers crossing the Channel disembarking on Utah, as had occurred on Omaha, the D-Day beach scene so horrifically depicted in *Saving Private Ryan*. As Dutch and the 505 started toward the Montebourg Station area, they were attacked, and the stress of killing was apparent.

---

5. Ryan, "Schultz interview," 3–4.
6. Ambrose, "Schultz," 11.

> Dutch: I ran by a wounded German soldier lying alongside of a hedgerow. He was obviously in a great deal of pain and crying for help. For some unknown reason, I stopped running about ten yards away from him and turned around. A close friend of mine was prodding this wounded man with his rifle and asking him if he had a pistol. The German was still crying when my friend put the muzzle of his rifle between the German's eyes and pulled the trigger. There was no change in my friend's facial expression. I don't believe he even blinked an eye. I was both appalled and awed by what I saw. Yet, there was a part of me that wanted to be just as ruthless as my friend. I thought this was a mark of a good paratrooper . . . (I came to realize that 'there but for the grace of God go I").

The celluloid version of Dutch Schultz's Normandy war was inaccurate. Dutch had not only been at Ste. Mere Eglise and La Fiere, he had been fighting for days and was baptized in the horrors of war. Extreme pain dogged him. On June 16th, he was removed from combat for a short period. D-Day's rough landing and his wrenched back had finally rendered him unable to walk.

> Dutch: At first, I had no back pain to speak of . . . even though I landed flat on my back with all of this equipment. And ten days later, my back was so injured and painful that I couldn't walk and ultimately was evacuated. My back started hurting me, I suppose, on the fourth or fifth day in Normandy and after I was starting to get adjusted to the combat situation.

Hospitalized in Cardiff, Wales, for a week, he quickly rejoined the 82nd and remained in battle until mid-July 1944.[7]

The 82nd had taken many losses in Normandy. Thirty-three days of action without relief or replacements, every mission accomplished, and no ground gained was ever relinquished. During these 33 days of combat, the 82nd Airborne was credited with destroying the fighting

---

7. Stephen Ambrose, "Schultz—Normandy Campaign June 7–June 14, 1944," Kalikow Collection, National WWII Museum, New Orleans, LA, 4, 6.

force of two German Infantry Divisions, but with their success, there was a heavy price. Of the entire group of the 82nd Airborne "All-American" Division who had come to Normandy by parachute, glider, or landing craft, only forty-two percent of them were not killed, wounded, or missing in action.[8]

My father's next combat experience, Market Garden, also has a historical presence in the retelling of World War II, but I never quite understood its goals or significance. The name of the operation conjured in my mind pleasant images of a bustling farmer's market somewhere in Holland. However, Market Garden was far from a pleasant affair. On September 17, 1944, thousands of American paratroopers were dropped in the Netherlands. Once there, they seized bridges at Eindhoven and Nijmegen, sustaining heavy casualties during their actions. Unfortunately, the American losses were in vain. British paratrooper counterparts were dropped at Arnheim, near the Rhine River border with Germany, their ultimate goal being to capture the final bridge into Deutschland, dubbed in another Cornelius Ryan book as *A Bridge Too Far*. Unfortunately, multiple failures by high command left the English troopers bogged down for over a week, and they finally surrendered to the Germans on September 25, 1944. Market Garden was a failure. The German homeland was not breached, and my father's war was fated to continue.[9]

Dad did not share much about his experiences at Market Garden; he always talked more about D-Day and the Bulge. All I knew was that he had carried a BAR on the jump into Groesbeck, Holland had a soft landing on a sunny September afternoon, and that the Dutch people were friendly and welcoming. After I read a portion of Stephen Ambrose's *Citizen Soldier*, I realized the emotional toll that the operation had taken on Dad. He had lost his role model, his company commander. Captain Anthony Stefanich had gathered Dad and other troopers to help soldiers on a crashed glider drawing enemy fire. Captain Stef was shot during the recovery mission. Death occurred within minutes while my father stood by him, crying and frantically praying the rosary. Dad was heartbroken. By the end of the Market Garden campaign in mid-November 1944, with the loss of his beloved captain, my father had become a

---

8. Bart Hagerman, USA Airborne: 50th Anniversary (New York: Turner Publishing, 1990), 162.

9. Geoffrey C. Ward and Ken Burns, *The War: An Intimate History 1941–1945* (New York: Alfred A. Knopf, 2007), 267–74.

battle-hardened man who had learned to suppress emotional responses to death and destruction.

> Dutch: It was not only a devastating loss for us, but the regiment as well. He was a born leader who led by example, not by virtue of rank. To the men of C Company, he was both our leader and friend . . . I felt like I lost an older brother. He was what I would have wanted to be when I finally grew up. It was the only time in combat that I broke down and wept over somebody that I cared about . . . a close friend of mine, Pvt Walter Faranfontoff, was killed a week later—while I mourned his loss, there were no tears.

The 505 remained in Holland until November, when they returned to Rheims, France.[10]

Dutch and the rest of his division didn't have much time to regroup after Market Garden. The surprise attack by the Germans in the Ardennes, or The Battle of the Bulge, haunted my father for the remainder of his life. The 82nd was on R and R in Rheims, France, in December while Hitler was planning a stealth counteroffensive against Allied troops in Belgium and Luxembourg. On a snowy December 16, 1944, the Fuhrer's scheme reached fruition. Thirty German divisions, including the elite Panzers, attacked a thinly defended Siegfried Line, a remnant of World War I. The 82nd was quickly called back to action, arriving in Werbomont, Belgium, on December 18, 1944.[11]

> Dutch: On December 18, we were awakened and told to get ready to leave by 0900 hours for a place called the Ardennes. I didn't have an overcoat, so I took a sleeping bag and made an outer garment of it. I put on some long johns, a GI sweater, a wool British Army garrison jacket and my jumpsuit . . . I believe I was still wearing my original jump boots. We didn't get the combat boots until later on in the Bulge . . . I didn't forget my insurance policy (my rosary, which I wore around my neck).

---

10. Stephen Ambrose, "Schultz—Holland Campaign," Kalikow Collection, National WWII Museum, New Orleans, LA, 4.

11. Gerald Devlin, *Paratrooper! The Saga of U.S. Army and Marine Parachute and Glider Combat Troops During World War II* (New York: St. Martin's Press, 1979), 521.

Facing horrendous fighting and shelling, the Germans surrounding my father's regiment, death was omnipresent.

Dutch was out of action for a while, hospitalized on Christmas Day 1944, until January 8, 1945, with severe pneumonia and dysentery. When he returned to "C" company, he came back to a unit that had been decimated. There was an achingly high rate of death and casualty.

> Dutch: I reported for duty to a company that was virtually
> wiped out. The officers were all gone, and we had about 30 men
> left. If I could have cried, I might have gotten some of the pain
> and guilt out. I lost some good friends who taught me how to
> survive in combat and often inspired me with their courage and
> sacrifice . . . In a larger sense, I realized the C Company I came
> to know and love no longer existed. The leadership that showed
> us how to reach beyond our limits and go to where we had
> never been was now gone.

The 505th regiment, of which company "C" was a part, lost over fifty percent of its men during the two weeks that my father was out of action. Replacement troopers were brought in to replace the many wounded and dead.[12]

As fighting waned, paratroopers were brought into the Belgian town of Theux in mid-January 1945 and placed in local households so they could finally bathe and eat. These men had gone a month without washing, surviving on cold field rations and living in foxholes without winter coats, and the warmth of the Belgian family, even for just a few weeks, was a bright spot in his cold, bleak winter. By late January, the 82nd was back in battle.

Early in February 1945, the division arrived at a scene my father described as resembling Dante's Inferno—the Huertgen Forest in the Ardennes along the Belgian-German border. In those dark woods, which resembled dark fairy tale scenes of Hansel and Gretel, catastrophic losses had befallen the American Army in November 1944. As Dad and his fellow troopers marched through the killing field, the snow was slowly

---

12. Phil Nordyke, *Four Stars of Valor: The Combat History of the 505th Parachute Infantry Regiment in World War II* (St. Paul, MN: Zenith Press, 2006), 377.

melting, and the "Bloody Huertgen" was giving up its dead. Body parts
were visible. Hundreds of corpses, tank hulks, and all manner of war
detritus had been left behind for months. The majority of dead and de-
composed were part of the 28th Infantry Division of the Pennsylvania
National Guard, a unit demolished by heavy German shelling, mines
and snipers. Gerald Astor in *The Bloody Forest* estimated the casualty toll
from Huertgen to be 24,000, a battle considered to be a military failure
that went unnoticed by the brass and press.[13] It was not unnoticed by
Dutch, however. He had never witnessed such carnage and inhumanity.
The odor from the decaying flesh was overpowering, and in his ill and
exhausted state, my father collapsed and lay on the side of the road.

> Dutch: The path that we were using had recently been cleared
> of mines by the engineers. However, there were still mines on
> both sides of the path, so it became crucial that you didn't stray
> too far from the center of the path . . . I became violently ill
> and fell to the ground. I laid there, not caring whether I lived or
> died. A first lieutenant helped me to my feet.

This unknown lieutenant dragged Dutch a mile to an aid station,
saving his life since he had double pneumonia and would have died from
exposure if left in the cold woods.[14] My father's harkening back to this
incident during the Bulge, shortly before his 2005 death, was telling.
Sixty years later, the horror of the winter of 1945 was still at the forefront
of his emotions.

After the Americans broke through the Bulge into Germany, the
paratrooper regiment was positioned in Northern Germany. Dutch had
been hospitalized again with pneumonia and rejoined his unit.

> Dutch: They were living in several houses facing the Rhine
> River near Cologne, Germany. On the day of my arrival, I was
> driven up to an area about a quarter of a mile of where my com-
> pany was actually located. While walking toward the company,

---

13. Gerald Astor, *The Bloody Forest: Battle for the Huertgen* (Novato, CA: Presidio Press, 2000), 338.
14. Dutch Schultz, "Dark Forest, Drop Zone Virtual Museum," accessed July 27, 2011, http://www.
thedropzone.org/europe.Germany/germanydefault.html.

I saw a GI who appeared to be hiding behind one of the houses and, every so often, he would look around the side of the house toward the river. When I got closer, I saw that he was a second lieutenant (apparently a recent replacement). I asked him where the company headquarters were located. After reporting in for duty, I commented to one of the men in the office about the lieutenant hiding behind one of the houses. He told me that one of our men had been killed at that location by a sniper the day before. I couldn't believe that this 2nd. Lt. would use me as bait to test the water. From that point on, I never turned my back on this guy, especially in combat. Thank God! He wasn't in my platoon.[15]

Dutch continued stoically throughout the remainder of the war. In the final days of the European Campaign, late April 1945, 505's C Company was pegged to spearhead an assault across the twelve-hundred-foot Elbe River into Bledecke, Germany. The prospect of crossing in small canvas/wooden boats while exposed to mortar fire raised the anxiety level of the unit.

Dutch: The longer we were exposed to combat, the more we felt like fugitives from the law of averages. In addition to all of the other combat risks of the past, we now faced the possibility of drowning . . . I was going to be the battalion commander's bodyguard . . . this was the first time that any of our battalion commanders had used a bodyguard . . . I knew that I didn't like him . . . After leaving shore, our fearless leader was urging us to paddle faster. He sounded like a coxswain counting cadence for one of the Ivy League rowing teams. At mid-river, it started snowing . . . we collided with another boat, which led to a shouting match about who had the right of way. It had to be the grace of God that guided us to the other side.[16]

---

15. Stephen Ambrose, "Schultz—Rhine River Campaign," Kalikow Collection, National WWII Museum, New Orleans, LA, 1.
16. Nordyke, 396.

Once in Germany, C Company was moving inland. Dutch directly confronted the enemy after diving into a ditch for cover from small arms fire and heavy 20mm explosions.

> Dutch: Upon jumping into it, I saw a German soldier who wasn't much more than sixteen years of age. We were about ten feet apart, with both of our weapons aimed at each other. In a few seconds, he dropped his rifle and raised his hands over his head. I never understood why I didn't shoot him the moment I saw him. I had been told many times to shoot first and ask questions later.

Later in the day, the Germans and C Company had a final skirmish.

> Dutch: We were still mopping up when a German machine gun opened fire on us from a nearby wooded area. For the sake of glory, I decided to go after it with hand grenades. After running into the woods and crawling about fifty feet in the general direction of the machine gun, I suddenly thought, 'why in the hell am I doing this?" Without so much as a second thought, I retraced my steps and rejoined my platoon. This abortive attempt to be a hero ended my combat career in the European Theater of Operations. A week later, the war was officially over, but not before the German 21st Army, consisting of 100,000 troops, surrendered to our Division.[17]

Before that surrender by Germany, the abject horror and brutality of the Nazi regime had been revealed to the 82nd. On May 2, 1945, paratroopers discovered the Wobbelin concentration camp, holding about 3,000 survivors when the soldiers arrived. Wobbelin was a repository where Nazis hid prisoners evacuated from two larger camps, Neuengamme and Ravensbruck. The sole reason for the existence of Wobbelin was to evade the liberation of the prisoners by the Allies. Four thousand prisoners had been transported and living in conditions even more primitive than those of the larger camps. One thousand corpses were

---

17. Nordyke, 402.

discovered by the soldiers of the 82nd and the 8th Infantry Divisions.[18] Starvation was prevalent; there were rumors that some prisoners had resorted to cannibalism.[19] Dad had never mentioned the camp until I asked him offhandedly in 2004 if he had ever been near a concentration camp. To my surprise, he told me of the 82nd's liberation of Wobbelin, that he still remembered the smell of the camp and then said no more. The specter of Wobbelin remained with him, however. In a later conversation, he reluctantly described the camp:

> Living skeletons were scattered about. It was difficult to distinguish the living from the dead. We forced the German population from the various towns around the camp to dig graves and bury over 200 bodies in front of a castle in Ludwigslust. If we ever needed a reason for fighting a war—this was it.[20]

After the German surrender on May 7, 1945, Dutch remained with his division in Germany until early December, when he returned to the United States, ready to begin the rest of his life. He planned to marry the girl in Philadelphia whom he had met on leave in 1942 and whose letters sustained him during the long years of the war.

But the soldier coming home was no longer a carefree, happy boy with big dreams of a major league career. He was a man who had been profoundly affected by war. My father's battle to integrate his warm nature with the horrors he had seen at war would last all his life. The legacy of World War II would not be the stuff of myth for his family even though to some, Dutch Schultz, the World War II paratrooper, is a mythic figure. Reenactors of that historic war contact me for permission to portray him in their battle games. Historians have quoted him and described his battle experiences. War movie buffs recognize his name and tell me he was a childhood hero of theirs, to some, the face of the American paratrooper in World War II.

To me, his daughter, the myth is bittersweet. During my childhood, I knew my Dad had been a paratrooper—his right hand sported a large

---

18. Nordyke, 403–405.
19. United States Holocaust Memorial Museum, Holocaust Encyclopedia, "Wobbelin," accessed July 27, 2011, http://www.usmm.org/wlc/en/article.php? ModuleId = 10006160.
20. Carol Schultz Vento interview of Arthur Schultz, August 2005.

gold ring with a parachute and the words 82nd Airborne. However, I never saw any other war memorabilia, even though he had been awarded two Purple Hearts and a Bronze Star. It would be decades before I laid eyes on the medals and awards—not until the 1990s, in the California home he shared with his third wife. His Silver Lakes bedroom was a shrine to his war with medals, decoratively colored aiguillettes and lanyards from America, France, Belgium and the Netherlands adorning the wall. Multiple decoupaged newspaper articles about Dad's exploits were prominently displayed. To complete the effect, a miniature white parachute hung from the ceiling. This display was in sharp contrast to my youth. During my childhood, World War II was subtly buzzing in the background, part of the story of how my parents met and the reason why Daddy taught me how to fight boys who picked on me. It was certainly not a topic of discussion at our dinner table. During the 1950s, my father wanted to forget. The same war that preserved his historic legacy also cut a swath of suffering and silence through my life.[21]

21. Page 40 has a pictorial and written list of Arthur Dutch Schultz's war honors prepared by Donald van den Bogert—www.pararesearchteam.com.

Arthur 'Dutch' Schultz – Personal Medals and Awards

1 Bronze Star Medal – for meritorious achievement against the enemy during the Normandy campaign in France.

2 Purple Hearts – 2 – Oak leaf cluster Normandy jump back injury; shrapnel wound left hand French Liberation Medal for jumping into Normandy – received 2000. A Headquarters Memo for one of the Purple Hearts reads: Arthur B. Schultz for wounds received as a result of enemy action on 6 June 1944 in the Normandy area, France

Combat Infantry Badge
The CIB is the metal badge award with the rifle on a blue background. This individual award is issued after the 1st combat action of an individual soldier. This award was listed in regimental orders, for issuing to the troopers, by chain of command (normaly the commanding officer).

3 European Campaign Medal
Decoration was intended to recognize those military service members who had performed military duty in the European Theater (to include North Africa and the Middle East) during the years of the Second World War. Colored bands representing Germany (on the ribbon's right), Italy (ribbon's left side), and the United States (center of the ribbon) are visible on the ribbon. The brown and green areas of the ribbon represent the terrain of the area of conflict, which ranged from beaches and sand, to grass and woodlands, to mountains.

4 American Campaign Medal
To be awarded the American Campaign Medal, a service member was required to either perform one year of duty (cumulative) within the continental borders of the United States, or perform 30 days consecutive/60 non-consecutive days of duty outside the borders of the United States but within the American Theater of Operations.
* TRAINED in the US, most Paratroopers received this medal.

UNIT CITATIONS (awarded to the 82nd A/B Division or 505th PIR)

Presidential Unit Citation with clusters.

Distinguished Unit Badge to 505th Parachute Infantry Regiment with streamer embroidered "Njimegen"
(this is an streamer awarded to the Regimental Flag)

Second Distinguished Unit Badge with streamer embroidered "Nijmegen"
(this is an streamer awarded to the Regimental Flag)

5 Decorative Cord – Order of William from Dutch – 82nd Airborne‡ only non Dutch division to receive it by Ministrial decree of the Dutch Minister of War, dated October 8, 1945, Section III A, Secret No-X 25

6 Decorative Cord – Belgian Croix de Guerre (6 = Scarlet Background with green) French Croix de Guerre (7 = Green background with red)
Belgian Cord by U.S. General Order #123 Headquarters 82nd Airborne Division

Army Parachutist Badge
Awarded to all military who complete Jumpschool signifies that the trooper is qualified to participate in airborne operations.

WWII Victory Medal, awarded to all US personnel who served on active duty, between Dec 7, 1941 / Dec 31, 1946.

NORMANDY 1944
Normandy Streamer for the 82nd AB. The Nijmegen and Ste Mere streamer are similar. All streamers are attached to the Divisional or Regimental Flag (based on the EAM Ribbon)

Arthur "Dutch" Schultz in 1942.

Dutch in Holland during WWII.

82nd Airborne in Cologne, Germany. Dutch is at front of truck on left.

Dutch during WWII.

3

GANGSTER AND HIS MOLL

I'll never smile again
Until I smile at you
I'll never laugh again
What good would it do?
For tears would fill my eyes
My heart would realize
That our romance is through

—"I'll Never Smile Again," Ruth Lowe, Songwriter

"What do you expect of parents named Dutch and Mitzi?" my sister would quip after yet another disastrous, post-divorce family episode. Their given names, Arthur and Madeline, were not much better as far as *normal* names go, but at least they had an air of dignity about them. Rosemary and I were embarrassed enough by our parents' split in the late 1950s without having to deal with parents who had nicknames similar to that of a mobster and his floozy, or in my mother's case, a small pampered dog.

We often wondered how the two of them had ever gotten together, our father an adventurous paratrooper whose family prided themselves on having "sand in their shoes," and our mother the youngest daughter of an immigrant family whose furthest move, after arriving in Philadelphia from Salerno, Italy, was to the next neighborhood over.

If World War II had not broken out, my parents would never have met. It was a typical, early 1940s tale—two young lovers thrown together by chance and circumstance. In 1942, my mother, Madeline (Mitzi) Russo, was a 21-year-old hairdresser who stopped by the local dry cleaners after work to chat with her girlfriend, Jane. Sitting on the counter with a broad smile, Army cap askew, and an attitude was a 19-year-old private visiting

Philly on leave. The cocky, young soldier had traveled to the East Coast city from Fort Story, Norfolk, Virginia, with his Army buddy, "Spags," a Philadelphia neighborhood boy. Later that evening, Mitzi got a pleading phone call from Jane. Spags would not go out dancing with her unless my mother also went out with the newly smitten private, Dutch Schultz. Years later, even after the acrimony of their divorce, Dutch described his first love as a young beauty with large brown eyes, thick auburn hair, and a small but sexy frame. Despite their different backgrounds, an instant attraction flamed between the two young people, and Dutch vowed to come back to Philly when the war was over and marry his Mitzi. His last night of leave in Philadelphia was romantic. While Billie Holiday's "I'll be Seeing You" played in the background, Dutch told Mitzi, "I'm going to marry you someday, kid—please wait for me."

Like so many other couples living with the specter of possible loss, my parents felt an overwhelming sense of urgency to commit to each other. After just a few short visits with his girl in 1943, Dutch was shipped overseas. He had earned his paratrooper wings after rigorous training at Fort Benning and was on his way to Northern Ireland to join the 82nd Airborne as a replacement. During his two-year absence, while he was engaged in brutal combat in Europe, Mitzi wrote to Dutch religiously and promised she would be there when he returned. Return he did in early December of 1945, but the irrepressible boy of 1942 had been replaced by a somber, melancholy man of twenty-two, relatively whole in body but riddled with psychological wounds from the carnage, death and destruction that he had experienced. Dutch, like so many other returning veterans, wanted nothing more than stability and a family, so he convinced Mitzi to plan quickly a traditional wedding for December 22.

The ceremony was performed at Mater Dolorosa Catholic Church, an Italian speaking parish in a row house Philadelphia neighborhood. Dutch looked extremely handsome in his paratrooper dress uniform, and Mitzi shone resplendent in a satin gown. The disparity in ethnicity and height between Dutch and the rest of the wedding party was striking. The groom, six feet tall, towered over the rest of the wedding party, none who topped five feet four. Dutch's family had moved from Detroit to the West coast during the war years, so most of the wedding party and guests were family and friends of my mother, short, dark and of Italian

heritage. Dad was a stranger in more ways than one, exemplified by my
Neapolitan grandmother's term for him, "The Medican," her attempt at
the English pronunciation of "American."

My father's "American" journey had begun when his twenty-four-
year-old consumptive mother gave birth to him in the Sonoran desert
city of Phoenix in 1923. Lucille, a spunky, motherless daughter of a
Colorado frontier homesteader, had moved to the young state of Arizona
with her second husband, Fred Schultz, a shell-shocked Marine veteran
of World War I, also plagued with tuberculosis. Lucille, an Army nurse,
had caught the disease tending to sick veterans, including Fred, at a sanitarium in New Mexico. The move to the dry desert air was to improve
their health and prepare for the birth of their baby.

Arthur Bernard Schultz entered the world at Saint Joseph's, the only
hospital in Phoenix. Being a nurse, his mother had progressive views and
shunned a home birth. The newborn came home to a two-room bunga-
low but was often kept separate from his parents as protection from their
tuberculosis. Often solitary, with only a neighbor woman who fed and
changed him for company, Arthur's infanthood was his first experience
with aloneness.

In 1925, the small family moved to the Rocky Mountain steel town
of Pueblo, Colorado, in the shadow of Pike's Peak. They lived with Frank
Barge, Lucille's distant father, a foreman for the Santa Fe railroad, who
was missing a limb due to a work accident. Frank had lost his first wife,
Martha Ellen, to cancer when Lucille was ten. Upon his remarriage to a
dour, cold woman also named Martha, Lucille and her younger brother
Bryant were placed in an orphanage by Frank who retrieved them in
the summer months. During warmer weather, the two Barge children
accompanied Frank on Santa Fe's western railroading routes. Lucille's
return to Colorado with Fred was not only to reunite with her father but
also to have a home for the young family while they looked for work.

The family's stay in Colorado lasted three years, during which another son, Ronald, was born. By 1928, the decision had been made to
move the family eastward to the bustling city of Detroit, Michigan,
where manufacturing jobs were plentiful.

The working class "Motor City" was Arthur's childhood home, from
kindergarten all the way through high school graduation. Detroit, with a

population of one million in the late 1920s, was the automotive capital of the world. More than half of the world's cars were built in its factories. During Dutch's childhood, the city's skyscape was opaque, with soot and grit belching from the factory stacks. Manufacturing plants littered the city's 144 square miles, and Fred Schultz found a steady job at the Budd Wheel plant. Steel automotive bodies were rapidly replacing the wood frames of the early cars, and Budd's early innovation in this type of design and manufacture guaranteed the company robust business from the likes of Dodge, Ford, Buick and Studebaker. Nursing jobs were also plentiful in Detroit, and Lucille easily found gainful employment as well. As an early dual-income couple, Lucille and Fred managed to avoid the ravages of the Depression.

It was here was christened "Dutch" by his boyhood friends, after the Roaring Twenties New York gangster and bootlegger Dutch Schultz, aka Arthur Flegenheimer. Dutch was no gangster, but he was a bit mischievous and led a pack of boys who often surprised neighborhood mothers with presents of garter snakes or frogs.

The metropolis of Detroit did not have the cachet of New York, but it was a bustling city with burlesque houses, movie theaters and sporting activities. In baseball, the Detroit Tigers, with Hall of Famers Hank Greenberg and Mickey Cochran, won the World Series in 1935 against the rival Cubs in six games. Their new professional football team, the Lions, won the NFL Championship in 1935, their second season in Detroit, after their move from Portsmouth, Ohio.

The Schultz residence consisted of six rooms in the upper half of a two-family flat, and was located on the east side of Detroit, an area comprised of mainly Irish and Italian working-class families. There were six rooms for six people, as two younger sisters, Mary Ann and Elizabeth, had been added to the family in the early Detroit years. Dutch was a student at Saint Philip Neri, a Catholic school, where the nuns tried in vain to break him of his independent and inquisitive ways. Corporal punishment was a daily ritual during his school years. Sometimes, in anticipation of a certain beating, Dutch would wear two sets of pants to soften the blows.

During his teenage years, Dutch's athletic skills were honed. Activities included lifeguarding and hockey games with teams in Windsor,

Canada. On the golf course at the swanky Country Club of Detroit in Grosse Pointe, he caddied for the likes of Edsel Ford, a dour, taciturn penny-pincher, and the tall, stylish car designer, Harley Earl, a gregarious and generous man. Dutch was the team captain for the baseball and basketball teams in high school. An outstanding first baseman, he had the highest individual batting average for all three baseball varsity years. He toughened up by boxing at Saint Rose's parish club at fourteen. By lying about his age, he competed successfully at fifteen in the Golden Gloves and won a Diamond Belt, the mark of an amateur boxing champion. Dutch Schultz seldom lost a fight on the street corner either. My gun-toting, frontier-bred grandmother encouraged her son's pugilism. She trained him to have the best left hook in the neighborhood, cautioning him never to run away from a fight. That was a needless admonition. Dutch's competitive spirit ensured that he would always persevere. The image of the teenage Dutch that persists in my mind is a carefree, handsome young man with amazing athletic skills and extraordinary self-confidence.

After graduating from Saint Philip Neri high school in 1941, Dutch visited his grandmother in New Mexico, planning to eventually return for college, a baseball scholarship waiting for him at Eastern Michigan University in Ypsilanti. However, the outdoors won him over that summer, and while in Santa Fe, he joined the Civilian Conservation Corps (CCC), a New Deal program that beautified the natural environment and created jobs for millions of unmarried, unemployed, able-bodied young men during the Depression years. The CCC approached its maturity in the late thirties and early forties. Thousands of young men participated in the program across the nation and lived together in barracks. Life in the camps followed a routine. Work was the order of every day, except Sunday, and after the evening meal, the men relaxed and had fun. Dutch ran the canteen/PX in his camp, a combined dayroom and recreation center.

In this building, amid the din of Ping-Pong, poker, bottles of coke, and occasional beers, friendships were fostered between young men of different backgrounds. Dutch's closest friends were teenage boys of Mexican descent, whom he stood up for more than once when the townies taunted them. Ironically, the CCC was a perfect training ground for military camaraderie and discipline, which would be needed for World War II, but that was still months away.

For the time being, eighteen-year-old Dutch was happy. He had big dreams for the future, which he was sure included a major-league baseball career. Then, on December 7, 1941, the course of my father's life changed forever and ultimately set the stage for mine.

His young wife's upbringing was a microcosm of the émigré experience in America. Mitzi, christened Madeline, was the youngest of four children to Italian immigrants, normally a favored position, but she grew up in a fractured family. Her father, Luigi Russo, had died at 32 after lingering for six painful months at the Pennsylvania Hamburg Sanitarium, a state-run hospital for tubercular patients. Madeline's role changed dramatically after her father's death. After Luigi died in 1923, her mother, Michelina, became the sole breadwinner for her children, who ranged in age from two to nine years. As a skilled seamstress, she quickly obtained a job in the bustling Philadelphia textile industry. Work was physically arduous. As a specialty sample maker in a factory churning out children's clothes, she toiled long hours. For extra money, Michelina would bring home piece work. In the evenings, the children would help her sew covers on baseballs. Michelina was a diminutive woman with a heavy accent and a strong will. She did what was necessary to keep her children together with her. She often sent Mitzi to her older sister's house in the Little Italy section of South Philadelphia. Giovanna, called Jenny, had a husband and a large brood of her own. Jenny and her husband operated a corner store, which enabled them to put the children to work while keeping an eye on them.

In spite of spending summers away from home, Mitzi maintained a close bond with her mother. Michelina controlled all her children with an iron hand, even into their adult years. She strongly disapproved of Mitzi's infatuation with Dutch because he was not of Italian heritage, not from the neighborhood or even the city. He had family, whom nobody had ever met, on the other side of the continent. Michelina was a strong believer in *la famiglia*. Like many Italian immigrants of the early twentieth century, my grandmother's "trust only the family" philosophy was formed not only by that Southern Italian character trait but also from personal experience. America did not provide a safety net for young widows, and the only aid Michelina received in her struggle to raise her four children was from her family.

It didn't take long for reality and major cultural differences to collide with the idealized images the bride and groom had of each other during the war. Mitzi had glorified Dutch as a handsome, exciting, and brave war hero, evidenced by his bronze star and two purple hearts. In her fantasies, he was going to rescue her from a restrictive environment and a home life that had grown increasingly tense due to the addition of her new stepfather. Dutch, during his long, dark days of combat, had held on to the dream of coming home to his beautiful, sexy, young girlfriend who would meet his every need. What they didn't count on was that while Dutch had physically left the war, it continued to rage on inside him. The first indication of trouble was the flask of liquor that he carried on the honeymoon train ride to see Dutch's parents in San Francisco. Dutch took long swigs from the flask buried in his coat. While they waited to switch trains in Chicago, the bottle dropped from his pocket and broke. As time went by, Dutch's need for alcohol grew stronger and more constant. Alcohol helped him sleep, not quite as haunted by the terrifying nightmares that had begun a few weeks after he left Europe. There was no way for either of my parents to know that Dutch was not alone, choosing alcohol to escape the war within him. The same scene played out in millions of veterans' homes all across the country. There was no diagnosis called post-traumatic stress disorder in 1945. Society accepted that World War II veterans sometimes suffered from a condition called combat fatigue, with rest and relaxation as the cure. According to postwar conventional wisdom, a real man would not be plagued by emotions of anxiety, fear and depression for very long. Dutch's struggles were emblematic of the combat soldier's homecoming struggles.

> Dutch: My first weeks at home were full of torment as I tried to forget my experiences in combat. I drank to forget until I was tired enough to sleep, only to be awakened by terrifying dreams and find myself bathed in sweat.[1]

---

1. Arthur B. Schultz, Veterans Administration file, 1946–2003.

Mitzi felt isolated and received no understanding about her dilemma from others, especially her immigrant mother. Dutch had come home a different man. Before the war, he was always laughing and talking, but when he returned, he was silent and somber. Michelina said that he was too quiet, and he was. He only talked to Mitzi about the horrors he had seen. It was she who soothed him in the dark.

Veterans with psychological wounds from World War II were consistently ignored. The stigma of being labeled as having an emotional problem prevented them from seeking treatment. Those who did seek help were told to "get over it" and readjust. It was not until 1980, in response to the pervasive and continuing mental health problems of Vietnam veterans, that the diagnosis of post-traumatic stress disorder was recognized by the American Psychiatric Association.[2] That was too late for my father and thousands of other vets, who had begun the process of self-medicating with alcohol. Alcohol abuse throughout the postwar population was a significant, although largely unacknowledged, characteristic of American family life. The World War II veterans appeased their demons with drink.

During my parents' honeymoon stay in California, they began to deal with the difficult transition from war to peace.

> Mitzi: He would have horrible nightmares. Still asleep, he frantically ran around the room, yelling, "Here they come! Get them!" Holding an imaginary gun, he would run to the window. I would touch him and try to soothe him, to tell him where he was and he was OK. Other nights, he would sweat so much that the mattress and my nightgown were soaked.[3]

Dutch drank and drank, only happy when he spent evenings with other paratroopers. These men, all veterans of sustained combat, imbibed all night, talking incessantly about the war, while the young wives waited impatiently to take their inebriated husbands home in the wee hours of the morning. Not totally understanding Dutch's invisible wounds, Mitzi, the sheltered baby of the family, soon got lonely and felt isolated. She

2. American Psychiatric Association (1980) *Diagnostic and Statistical Manual of Mental Disorders* (3rd ed) (DSM—III). Washington, DC: APA.

3. Carol Schultz Vento interview with Madeline Schultz Bondy, February 2, 2009.

wanted to return to Philadelphia to live. Dutch had made that promise when she agreed to his marriage proposal, but he had had a change of heart. He wanted to remain in California. He was attending college at San Francisco State and playing on their varsity baseball team, an attempt to recapture his lost youth and deferred dreams. At an impasse, my parents decided to separate. Dutch took Mitzi to the San Francisco station and put her on the train going east alone. It seemed that my parents were going to become part of the booming postwar divorce rate.

Divorce was their plan. The hasty postwar marriage seemed as if it was headed for failure, but then I intervened—completely unplanned. Mitzi felt increasingly nauseous on the long, bumpy train ride back to Philadelphia. She initially thought her discomfort was due to stress from the quick demise of her new marriage. However, when her nausea did not subside, she visited the doctor and discovered that she was pregnant. She didn't want Dutch to stay married to her out of obligation. She also had other options. Her older sister, Annie, had offered to share a small apartment with her in Philadelphia and assist in raising the baby. Dutch, however, was elated at my impending birth, a spark of life after the war's horror and death, and the couple soon reconciled. Mitzi took a plane back to California to join Dutch on a bicoastal trip back East. An elderly San Fran dowager needed to get a car to her son in Lancaster, Pennsylvania, and the soon-to-be parents made money driving cross country on two-lane highways back to the East Coast.

> Mitzi: I wanted to stay married, and I did at that time. I flew back to San Francisco because Dutchie wanted to finish his semester. It was a conundrum for me. He was in his environment and happy with his student friends. I was out of mine— the working world. What a dilemma. In June 1946, we drove home through flooded waters that were as high as Midwestern cornstalks, through sweltering summer heat. Morning sickness, frightening mountain paths, and finally home again to a rented little house, which we turned into a home with furniture donated by my family and a baby crib.[4]

---

4. Madeline Schultz Bondy, unpublished writing, May 5, 2005.

At a time before interstates were the norm, this continental trip took at least a week. During my mother's pregnancy with me, she had traveled across America three times, each trip entailing a different mode of transportation—train, plane, and automobile. Upon their arrival in Philadelphia, my parents moved into a working-class neighborhood. The house that they rented was shared with two of my mother's siblings, a common postwar occurrence, which was not particularly conducive to marital privacy but necessary because of Dutch's difficulty in getting work.

I was born full term in October 1946, a sickly, five-pound baby. My frail condition was probably due to the 9000 miles I had racked up prior to my birth. My parents' reconciliation before I was born has always been a source of guilt and ambivalence. With the conflict and tragedy that lay in their future, I wondered whether I was the only reason, in those early days, for the continuation of their marriage, a marriage that produced two subsequent children who died before their time and plenty of regret, recriminations, and sadness. In later years, both of my parents separately assured me that they were in love and wanted to work out their difficulties, not realizing the impossibility of the task. Neither of them recognized, in the 1940s, how the war had truly come home to stay. In a letter on their first anniversary, in December of 1946, Dutch tried to explain the unexplainable to his confused young wife:

> My dear wife, I am writing this letter with a heavy heart and a weak spirit because, for the first time in my life, I feel like a failure. My marriage to you was a dream come true, a dream I lived with for three years. When it came to fruition, that dream became a reality. To repeat what I told you, "A marriage made in heaven." The completion of this dream was for us to live on the West Coast, the open land where one enjoys the fresh, warm breeze the colorful landscape and have a great zest for living. This I want to share with you, not the grey skies, drab dull surroundings where people hibernate most of their lives. That is where we met the fork in the road. The piercing hurt of the decisions we must make. This is my future life. After years of restrictions, years of killing, fear and hiding, I want to be free to eat, sleep and, yes, live where I want to. We married in haste,

not that I regret it, but I feel bound, almost suffocated, reminding me again of the days I spent with Uncle Sam. I thought
my obligations and duties were over. I need time, time again to
adjust. I must find myself to make this marriage work. Remember, I love you and Carol very much. When I find myself, I will
be back. This back and forth I have done for years until I was
not there. I decided I must find myself. Until then, keep this
love I have for you in your heart forever.[5]

Dutch then moved out for about a month, but soon he was back.
Mitzi was pregnant again. Dutch re-entered the military on February 7,
1947, hoping to find job stability. After training at Fort Holabird, Mary-
land, for Army Counterintelligence, he was assigned to the Philadelphia
Counterintelligence Corps Office. Home with his family, he awaited the
birth of his second child. A girl, Mary Ann, was born in November 1947.
It was far from a joyous event. Two days later, Mary Ann died from a
brain deformity, Microencephaly.

Dutch: The attending doctor showed me the baby, born without the top of its head . . . My shock was too great . . . I never
got over it.[6]

Despite the loss of their second daughter and the attendant heartache,
the two of them remained together. Dutch was assigned to Germany for
language immersion and advanced counterintelligence training. One of
his instructors was Staff Sergeant and future Secretary of State Henry
Kissinger. When Dutch returned to Philadelphia in 1950, Mitzi again
became pregnant and a healthy baby, Rosemary, was born on April 10th,
1951. Shortly thereafter, Dutch was sent to Europe again, this time to
occupied Austria. As part of the 430th Army Counterintelligence Corps
detachment, at twenty-nine, Dutch became an agent in charge of the field
office at Zell Am See, a bucolic skiing village in the heart of the Bavarian
Alps, about thirty miles from Eagles Nest, Hitler's hideaway in Berchtes-
gaden, Germany. He was in charge of directing double agent operatives,

5. Letter from Arthur Schultz to Madeline Schultz, January 15, 1947.
6. Arthur B. Schultz, Veterans Administration file, 1946–2003.

a sensitive and stress-producing position. The family was together in Austria for a year before Mitzi, feeling alienated and alone again, wanted to
return home. Dutch returned six months later to Philadelphia, and once
again, tension in the marriage grew. In 1957, when Dutch volunteered
for Russian language training in preparation for another tour overseas,
Mitzi refused to follow him and asked for a divorce. Dutch fell to pieces.

> Dutch: The shock was too much, and I started to go to
> pieces . . . I cannot describe the sensations I had more than to
> say that I felt apart from anything real. On a five-day emer-
> gency leave for the purpose of solving my domestic difficulties,
> I went to a civilian doctor who immediately suggested I turn
> myself over to the military authorities. I needed his assistance
> to do this as I had broken down completely and was sobbing
> for extended periods of time. The psychiatrist at the military
> hospital who interviewed me gave me some tranquilizers and
> sent me home.[7]

This time, my parents' marriage was over. There was a short reconciliation after Dutch resigned from the military to try to save their marriage.
We moved to San Diego, near my paternal grandparents, for about six
months with the hope of a fresh start, but Dutch's drinking accelerated
after his breakdown. Mitzi lost patience and eventually took my sister
Rosemary and me back to Philadelphia, where she filed divorce papers.
A keepsake from my parents' time together sits in the back of my
closet, their large wedding photograph in an ornate ivory frame. When I
discovered it in my mother's closet two decades ago, flaking and battered,
I had it restored to its original condition. I had never been successful in
restoring their failed marriage, but I at least had tangible evidence of their
love for each other at one time. The hopeful bride, in her satin wedding
dress, heart-shaped neckline framing her beaming face, and the groom,
tall and resplendent in his dress paratrooper dress uniform bedecked with
decorations and medals, was to me a glimpse of what once was and could
have been if the horror of war had not intruded.

---

7. Arthur B. Schultz, Veterans Administration file, 1946–2003.

Arthur in Detroit in the late 1920's.

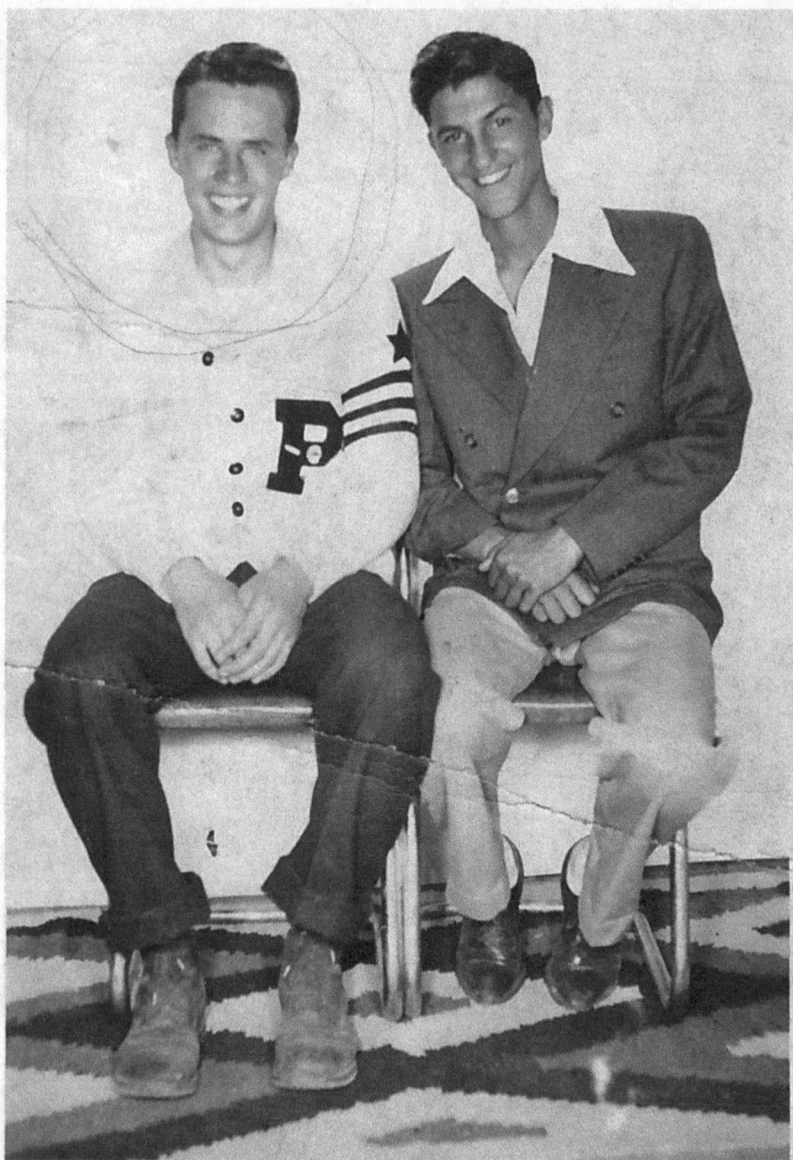

Dutch in high school.

Dutch at high school graduation in 1941.

Madeline Russo in 1941.

Dutch and Mitzi in 1942.

Arthur "Dutch" Schultz in paratrooper dress uniform, December, 1945.
(front cover photograph)

Wedding December 22, 1945.

4

THE LONGEST DAYS

Many men, the mighty thousands
Many men to victory
Marching on, right into battle
In the longest day in history

—Paul Anka, "The Longest Day"

The rising dead, faces bloated, torn
They are relieved, the living wait their turn
Your number's up, the bullet's got your name
You still go on to hell and back again

How long on this longest day
Till we finally make it through
How long on this longest day
Till we finally make it through

—Iron Maiden, "The Longest Day"

Red, wiry hair shot like flames from his scalp. Intensity and madness shone in his aquamarine eyes—his nose shaped like an upside-down question mark. Thin lips pressed together. Pale, ghostly complexion, translucent with prominent blue veins.

He was our twenty-ish, next-door neighbor, Jerry. He lived with his nervous, chain-smoking, gray-haired mother in the downstairs apartment of the dilapidated row house next door to us. The five-foot wooden plank fence, which separated our postage stamp yards, was no barrier to his passion. He was obsessed, burning with the fervency of a born-again Christian, for my newly divorced mother. His pitiful excuses for coming to our door with offerings of pies, cookies, and donuts were transparent.

He stood there staring at her with smoldering eyes, all the while regarding us with annoyance and disdain. His countenance darkened when we were in the house, and we could sense the dislike oozing from his pores like some noxious odor.

We called him Devil Man behind his back, in homage to both his personage and his character. He sensed our simmering antagonism and took an opportunity to mask his resentment through a supposed act of kindness towards me, which involved a "hair from hell" moment. He was a barber and promised me the latest chic haircut from the glossy pages of my favorite teen magazine. The result was less than promised. I was shorn so that I resembled a twelve-year-old boy with braced buckteeth and protruding ears. My thick, coarse, brown hair was plastered to my head and approximated the flat appearance of a male department store mannequin or a bobblehead doll. The razor that Devil Man wielded not only got rid of most of my hair, but obliterated my softly feminine young attractiveness. I was a contradiction, a stiff, unsmiling boy head with a developing, curvaceous body. Red-headed Jerry could barely disguise his glee at my mortification.

His presence in our lives ended frighteningly one summer evening after my mother broke off her relationship with him. Gun in hand, he walked into the beauty shop and growled to her, "If I can't have you, no one else can." As my sister and I were rushed upstairs by mom's friend, we overheard our mother's words to Devil Man, "Let's go out on the porch so the kids don't see you shoot me!" Police were soon at the scene and disarmed him peacefully.

Devil Man may have been the scariest new person in our lives, but we were adjusting to an ever-changing cast of characters. After our parents' divorce in March 1959, my mother converted our home into a combination beauty shop/boarding house. The only room off limits to strangers was our front bedroom. After Dad left, Mom, being Italian and over-protective, insisted that she and her two daughters must all sleep in that room, the one my sister and I had shared for years. A surplus army cot and a used gray bureau were stuffed into the boxy environ. My mother now used my twin bed. I had offered to sleep on the cot, imagining myself roughing it, just like Dad. At night, our bedroom door was double locked, sporting a deadbolt and chain, and our meek, aging collie, Rain, was left outside the "safe" room to protect us.

When my father lived with us, home life had a modicum of predict-ability. After he was gone, we never knew who would be populating the other two bedrooms. First in the parade of boarders was a soldier, his Japanese wife, and their pudgy baby. The one bathroom with its claw foot tub and small toilet was now in significant overuse. A thin elderly woman with tight salt and pepper curls that belied her warm demeanor was next. Always giving us candy treats, we quickly grew attached to Aunt Ellen. When she left, we were presented in rapid sequence with a pair of bookend boarders, two working-class ethnic women, one after the other. Mary was Italian; Pearl was Polish. They both cleaned our house obsessively, even though they paid rent, in hopes of getting my mother's approval.

In addition to the series of boarders, beauty shop customers overtook the remainder of our postage stamp house. The living room was trans-formed into a salon, with a beautician sink, helmet hair dryers, a Revlon nail and lipstick display, and the constant fumes of cold wave permanent and Aqua Net hairspray. The drywall separating the "shop" from our liv-ing area was painted a feminine mauve. A neon sign in our front window blinking "Mitzi's Beauty Shop" was lit day and night.

My mother wore a pure white uniform every day. She opened her shop at 7 AM; customers were already sitting on the porch every morn-ing waiting for her to unlock the door. They were weekly regulars in those days of roller sets, beehives, updos, and big bouffant hair, a la Jackie Kennedy, hair sprayed to last a week. Getting ready for school in the morning, I often had to compete for breakfast space at the kitchen table. The regulars brought creamy butter cake and powdered sugar donuts, and the ladies made coffee and ate pastries while I wolfed down my morning cereal.

Mom had to get money from the beauty shop and our boarders be-cause Dad's contribution to our family finances was irregular at best, even though he was employed. Right after the split, Dad was back at the Frankford Arsenal as a civilian employee, but he soon left for a high-profile position. The August 14, 1962, edition of the *Philadelphia Bul-letin* featured my father as a newly-hired Chief Investigator, for a grand jury probe of corruption in Philadelphia city government. The article highlighted Dad's credentials as an army counterintelligence agent in

Germany, Austria, and the States, in addition to his World War II para-trooper experience in Europe.[1] Unfortunately, within a few months, the Pennsylvania Supreme Court declared the grand jury and its investigation to be invalid. Suddenly unemployed, Dad and two partners formed a private detective agency in center-city Philadelphia, which was quite successful until Dad's problem with alcohol accelerated. He was soon in debt and used funds from the business for personal matters. The flurry of attention garnered by *The Longest Day* began to fade into the background. Rosemary and I were somewhat oblivious to our father's worsening problems. He had settled into a routine with us, taking us miniature golfing and swimming on the weekends and to the occasional weeknight movie.

This normalcy ended abruptly with Dad's sudden marriage to a fellow alcoholic. A leggy Italian brunette, Ardelle, was an underwear model who departed her New York career with a portfolio of modeling clips, a serious alcohol and drug problem, a history of mental breakdowns, and multiple suicide attempts. Unbeknownst to us, Dad's drinking was becoming uncontrolled at times. In 1963, he entered the Cutler Clinic of Wawa Hospital, a "drying out" center in Wawa, Pennsylvania, where Ardelle had already been an inpatient for a few weeks. Dad was quickly smitten by her looks. They married only two weeks after meeting, and the newly sober newlyweds took off for Florida.

Completely unaware that Dad had suddenly married, we were waiting on our stoop for him to pick us up when, in his stead, Joe appeared with news of the marriage. A month went by before Dad returned. When we finally met Ardelle at the couple's downtown Philly apartment, it was an awkward scene. She attempted to break the ice by showing us scrapbooks with revealing newspaper underwear shots of her. Eleven-year-old Rosemary and I squirmed, looking uncomfortably at the photos of Dad's new wife in panties and bra, unsure of how to respond.

After my father's remarriage, he slowly lost his way. Sobriety was short-lived both for him and Ardelle. Reeking of beer, he stumbled into our house for my "sweet sixteen" birthday party. The former boxing champion, well past his prime, challenged my friends to fight him. I was mortified, especially since my diminutive mother had already

---

1. "Grand Jury Investigator Won $2500, Then Lost It Before Jump on D-Day" *Philadelphia Bulletin*, August 14, 1962, 52.

embarrassed me when she had patted the boys as they arrived at the party, up and down their bodies for liquor bottles. I could hear my group of friends muttering in the background, "Her old man's a drunk."

My father's life continued downhill. His partnership with the private detective agency was lost because of his drinking and financial impropriety. He had sporadic contact with us, sometimes not appearing for planned visits. I arrived late to my senior prom because I kept waiting for Dad, who never showed up. Although I don't remember, I must have conveyed my disappointment to him because years later, I found a letter from November 1963:

> Dear Carol Ann: Am real sorry I couldn't share part of the night with you . . . . Until I can get my life in some order—I want . . . you to be patient with me. I, at the moment, have more problems than I ever thought possible. I need time to put these problems in some sort of direction. If I don't succeed in this—I am afraid everything will break down. I well understand your feeling that I am letting you down. My only thought to this—is that I am not doing it intentional.[2]

I remember feeling confused, sad, worried and also hurt by the lack of attention from the Dad who was previously so invested in me.

However, nothing prepared me for my father's phone call one bitter January night in 1964. I was home babysitting my sleeping sister. Unaware that Dad and Ardelle had returned to binge drinking, it was a shock for me to hear my father's slurred words, "Ardelle slit her wrists and she's bleeding in the bathtub." Sobbing, he told me that he had a gun in his hand and wanted to kill himself. I pleaded with him not to pull the trigger. Sitting on the green chenille couch, clenching the black rotary phone, I kept telling him he was a good father in between his frenetic repetition of "I missed the boat—I failed you girls." I sat frozen for a minute after he hung up. Then, Mom walked in and immediately called Dad back. Surprisingly, he picked up the phone, and she managed to calm him down a bit. Next, she called Joe, who quickly went to Dad's

---

2. Arthur Schultz to Carol Schultz, personal Letter, November 12, 1963, personal files of Carol Schultz Vento.

apartment, which was in shambles. Broken furniture was strewn about from Dad's alcoholic rampage. The bathroom was bloodstained from Ardelle's razor slashing. Dad was in the midst of a breakdown and needed a quick intervention. My grandmother wired money, and Joe put Dad on a plane to his parents' home in San Diego.

Both my sister and I were upset. I held my emotions in, and she took refuge in her diary:

> Rosemary, Age 12: It's completely awful about my father–awful. He called here last night. Carol got scared because he was crying and everything. He was drunk with his wife. He said he was leaving for Calif. Monday. I hope he does. Back to Grandmom. It's not fair. It's just not fair. Grandmom's not so young any-more. As I said before, I need a friend, so I am going to make you my best friend. And since all my friends have names, yours will be Melony, if you don't mind. I love that name.[3]

Ardelle, who had survived her latest suicide attempt, was institution-alized in late January at Norristown State Hospital, a mental hospital in the suburbs of Philadelphia. By early summer, Ardelle was deemed cured and released, whereupon she joined Dad in San Diego. The two of them lived together on my grandparents' property and attended Alcoholics Anonymous meetings nightly. Dad put all his energy into himself and limited contact with his daughters, except for the occasional letter de-tailing his struggles with sobriety and the difficulty of finding part-time work while he attended college on the GI bill. In a letter to the Veterans Administration in the spring of 1964, Dad was beseeching the govern-ment for help:

> I am attempting to obtain employment in San Diego, but so far, I have been unsuccessful. While my search for employment continues, I realize that employment in my field . . . will be extremely difficult to obtain because of my record for Alcohol-ism and also because of my poor credit rating . . . discovery of these facts will preclude my obtaining a job as a government

3. Rosemary Schultz, personal diary, 19 January 1964, personal files of Carol Schultz Vento.

employee in the field of intelligence or investigation. To sum up
the purpose of revealing my "fall from grace," I am requesting as
much assistance as I am allowed under the law so that I might
return to the status of a productive human being. I have hopes
of returning to school with the idea of obtaining a degree in
some field of endeavor that will allow me to work with people
afflicted with the disease of Alcoholism.[4]

In retrospect, I realize his survival was at stake, but back then, I felt
abandoned. Never even acknowledging my high school graduation, the
father who had been so proud of my intellectual abilities had left me to
navigate the college process alone in a family of Italians, none of whom
had gone beyond the tenth grade. I figured it out and kept my emotions
in tight control, vowing to be grown up and successful.

In 1967, I was a junior at Temple University in Philadelphia, working
my way through college, when a phantom walked by me on Broad Street,
the middle of the urban campus. It was my father. He passed by me
without even a flicker of recognition in his eyes. The man who had been
my best friend as a child didn't even know me and had not attempted to
contact me upon his return to the city. Too embarrassed to approach him
and ask if he was my father, I did nothing. Upon my return home, I told
my mother about the possible reappearance of my father. After contact-
ing Joe Tallett, mom confirmed that it was indeed Dad. My father, who
had almost self-exterminated, had come back from the brink and returned to Philadelphia. The years in California with his parents had given
him a refuge, even if he was living in a garage for part of the time. Armed
with his college degree, he was at Temple on an interview for graduate
school in psychology when he passed me by. Dad called later that evening
after talking to Joe. He and Ardelle had maintained their sobriety, and
now both of them had jobs as counselors at Eagleville Hospital, a former
tuberculosis sanitarium in suburban Philadelphia that had converted to
a treatment center for alcoholics in 1965, offering both detoxification
and rehabilitation services on an inpatient basis. Dad became director of
the men's program and Ardelle, the women's. Donald Ottenberg, MD,
Executive Director of the newly formed treatment hospital and Ardelle's

4. Arthur Schultz letter, April 5, 1964, Veterans Administration file of Arthur B. Schultz 1946–2004.

psychiatrist, was innovative in the alcohol recovery field and believed in hiring recovering alcoholics as staff members. As Director of the men's program, my father's previous career experience as a hard-nosed paratrooper and Army counterintelligence agent, coupled with the prevailing psychological method of the day, was a perfect fit. Encounter groups, an offshoot of Carl Rogers' group dynamics psychological model, were all the rage in the 1960s. Also known as sensitivity training or human development groups, the focus was on authenticity and true expression of emotion. The group leader, with assistance from other group members, was tasked with breaking down the defensive mechanisms of the participant, who was on the "hot seat."[5] In these group settings, Dad was able to release his inner master sergeant. With the prevalent motto of "letting it all hang out," the idea was to get results in an intense environment, which suited my father very well. Marathon groups, which applied encounter group principles over two days with a six-hour sleep break, were often used at Eagleville and led by my father. "Marathon Therapy: Effect as a Change Agent in the Treatment of Alcoholics and Drug Addicts" was the title of the thesis paper my father wrote to fulfill his requirements for a master's degree from Temple University, and his population studied consisted of members of ongoing Eagleville hospital therapy groups.[6]

With his success and continuing sobriety, Dad left Eagleville in 1971 to become director of a new program, Today, Inc., in Bucks County, Pennsylvania. "Today is the first day of the rest of your life" motto was in vogue during that seeking era, attributed to Charles Dederich, the founder of Synanon, a California drug rehabilitation program that focused on living the examined life. Regrettably, Synanon transformed into a cult in the 1970s and was closed down due to reports of criminal activities, but its influence on the behavior modification field, through the confrontation and encounter group model, lasted longer than the actual therapeutic program.[7]

Today was created by five Bucks County, Pennsylvania community leaders, whose vision was to have a residential rehab program for teenage

---

5. Irvin D. Yolom and Molyn Lesczc, *The Theory and Practice of Group Psychotherapy*, 5th edition (New York: Basic Books, 2005), 530.

6. Arthur B. Schultz, "Marathon Therapy: Effect as a Change Agent in the Treatment of Alcoholics and Drug Addicts" (Masters thesis, Temple University, March 1970).

7. "Synanon," Wikipedia, accessed August 3, 2011, http://en.wikipedia.org/wiki/Synanon.

substance abusers as an alternative to prison. Dad was a good fit for their model, which emphasized the confrontational approach. One of the creators of the Today program described Dad's technique as a "cross between Attila the Hun and Jesus Christ."[8] During their stay at Today, Dad and Ardelle lived on the program grounds and helped develop the model. After Dad was hired, Ardelle became the head of the women's section. While Today was flourishing, my father's second marriage was failing. The summer of 1973 brought another divorce for Dad, complicated by the necessity of a job change. He and Ardelle could not both remain in their positions. The reason why was never explained to me, but possibly the tension was too intense for both of them. Dad decided to leave, and Ardelle remained at Today until she committed suicide on January 21, 1974. She was 44 years old.

Starting over again at fifty, Dad gave Rosemary and me some of his furniture. In the summer of 1973, he packed up his RV trailer for a cross-country trip to Santee, California, near his younger sister. Without a permanent home once again, he planned to live in the RV until he figured out his next move.

8. William Eastburn III, Oral Statement at Arthur Schultz funeral, Arlington, VA, December 7, 2005.

Schultz family in 1949.

Schultz family, Zell am See, Austria, 1949.

Carol Schultz in 1957.

Dutch Schultz, 1957.

Madeline Russo, 1967.

5

LOST CHILD

Over time, I realized that my father was not alone in his defeat. There were many other vets like him, emotionally scarred by the "Good War," who failed to live up to the impossible standards set for men of their era. I was lucky, in fact, to be Dad's confidant. Most loved ones were kept in the dark. World War II vets are notoriously closemouthed, the stoic product of the Great Depression and wartime, when ideals of honor, courage, patriotism, sacrifice, and self-reliance fostered impregnable reticence.

—Julia Collins, *My Father's War*, p. 10

"Your daughter is dead."

—Philadelphia policeman to Mitzi Schultz,
11:58 PM, November 22, 1973

"We were supposed to grow old together," I said to my sister Rosemary that rainy November eve. She didn't answer. Lifeless in her white, satin-lined casket, she would never answer me again. I choked back tears, became rigid, and rejoined my parents in the somber reception line. Not exactly the type of greeting procession the two of them had expected to be in for their youngest daughter. Rather than accepting congratulations at her wedding, the two of them, physically closer to each other than they had been in a decade, greeted mourners at her viewing.

Thanksgiving night, November 22, 1973, just four days earlier, had found me overstuffed and sleepy in the Philadelphia apartment that I shared with my husband. Earlier that day, I bade goodbye to Rosemary as she left the traditional Italian family feast at our aunt's house. My sister's thin arms were wrapped tightly around her boyfriend's waist as he revved the motor on his black and silver Yamaha cycle and sped off.

I had more than a momentary worry. My twenty-two-year-old sister's latest choice in men was a disaster. She looked pale and tired. She worked long hours as a waitress at Khyber Pass, a trendy center-city Philly club, and juggled a full load of classes at Temple University. The heavy load was wearing her down. Tom (name changed), her boyfriend, had an air of lassitude about him. Long-haired and messy, his counterculture artist patina was belied by his oily manipulation. The lack of a male figure in our household had especially impacted Rosemary, only seven when my parents divorced, and left her vulnerable to the machinations of men like Tom. The scheme hatched by her current partner was to make money off of her—Rosemary would become a *Playboy* centerfold. Photos of her partially clothed were taken by Tom's professional photographer friend, Frank Bender, and mailed to Playboy headquarters. In September 1973, not surprisingly, she received an offer to fly to Playboy in Chicago to become a Playmate. My sister was the All-American girl with a killer figure. Blonde, blue-eyed and relatively tall, she had inherited the Irish-Scots-German genes that had missed me. Despite my angry protestations that she was being exploited, Rosemary had decided to accept the offer, telling me that she was mature enough to make her own decisions. However, she must have had second thoughts because she wrote to my father to ask for his opinion. Dad was now in Santee, California, living in his trailer in space 39. He gave Rosemary fatherly advice with caution since his paternal role had been fractured over the recent years.

> Dutch: Re: The *Playboy* thing—my question to you—is your head on tight? Because every "swinging dick" from Philadelphia to Chicago is going to try and get "into your drawers." Are you strong enough to withstand this kind of pressure? If so—do it and get the money, then "thumb your nose" at the *Playboy* philosophy. Be sure, though, that you know exactly what you are getting into. There are a lot of people in this world who can hurt you, especially if they are looking at you without your clothes on. I know you will make the right decision & I wish you much love and happiness. Work hard on your maturity. Love always, Dad.[1]

1. Arthur Schultz to Rosemary Schultz personal letter, September 10, 1973, personal files of Carol Schultz Vento.

While I did not dissuade her, the letter from Dad did the trick. Rosemary had not mentioned the *Playboy* offer to our mother, who would have fainted from shock and distress at the idea of her scantily clad daughter being displayed coast to coast. Rosemary had been looking for fatherly guidance and was slowly rebuilding a relationship with our father. Dad and I had a closer bond. I was the oldest, and he was around for more of my upbringing. When our parents divorced, Rosemary went into denial mode. A second grader at a Catholic school, she wanted to fit in and told her friends, for over a year, that her father was away in the Army. She was conflicted, to a greater degree than I, between loyalty to her mommy or Daddy. And mommy usually won out. Rosemary was unduly worried about our mother, whom we mainly depended upon for financial support. Her anxiety is evidenced by her diary:

> Rosemary, Age 12: I got a letter from the nurse today saying I didn't pass my eye examination. Mommy believed that I needed glasses now. I am going to help pay for them because Mommy doesn't have much money now. I wonder how Daddy is. We haven't heard from him yet.

Now, just as Rosie and Dad were finally getting closer, the chance to build on their relationship was taken away from him forever. I called him in the early morning hours of November 23rd and, with a choked voice, told him that his youngest daughter was dead. His wailing and sobbing chilled me, and I became more emotionally numb than I already was.

The accident that ended her life was not a total surprise. Tom was a careless driver. He had had a prior motorcycle accident with a female passenger who was seriously injured. In the accident that killed my sister, he suffered with no more than broken legs, recovered fully, and haunted our family's life for decades. He exploited my mother, often asking her for money when he was down and out. He told her he was a psychic and could reach across the veil of death to communicate with my dead sister. My grieving mother was an easy target for his ploy. Tom's manipulation ended only after my mother's remarriage, and my stepfather saw through the act and cut off all monetary assistance.

Back in the 1970s, there was an awareness that my sister's poor choices were influenced partly by our parents' divorce; however, there was no recognition that my father's war may have had something to do with our family's troubles. Rosemary died long before the term Post-Traumatic Stress Disorder became part of the descriptive vocabulary in America for soldiers who returned from war. It was not apparent that our father's scars had become her own. She kept it hidden, but she had picked up some suicidal ideation from him.

> Rosemary, 1970—I'd like to die—not that I would even kill myself, but I'm curious to know what happens . . . I'll study now so that I'll become "educated." And one day, my brain will rot in the ground along with billions of other people.[2]

This overachiever daughter, who graduated near the top of her high school class, won a scholarship to college and was noticed for her beauty, had kept her anxiety and depression a secret. World War II was a victorious war—why would the children of those warriors have any problems?

The chaos of living with a traumatized combat vet had not yet been studied. The Schultz family life can be viewed through the prism of the children. We coped with the fall out of war; alcoholism and divorces were part of our reality. Rosemary and I were casualties of Dad's war, but we each expressed it in different ways.

I was the prototypical rescuer, always ready to save my family members. My feelings were put on ice to deal with the drama and the more immediate emotional needs of other family members. During the turbulent late adolescent and early adult years of my sister's life, I was a surrogate parent, the one that she came to with her problems. My mother worked long hours in her beauty shop, and she had a busy social life with ballroom dancing and Single Parent events. My father was struggling to overcome his own demons, reinvent himself in a career, and deal with a difficult second marriage. My sister's reaction was more troubled. Despite her academic success in high school, she had difficulty focusing on her college studies. She moved out of our mother's apartment to stay with my father when he was directing the Today program. That move caused

---

2. Rosemary Schultz personal diary, May 6, 1970, personal files of Carol Schultz Vento.

more conflict within our family. Loyalty became an issue for both my parents. They competed for her, and each parent would get upset when she left one to stay with the other. Finally, she began a series of moves to apartments of her own. At the end of her life, she was living with Tom, having moved to his apartment only a few months before her death.

The years that Rosemary and I should have spent developing our separateness from our parents we were both held captive to the residuals of our father's war, unaware that his unseen scars had been passed down to us.

Acknowledgment of the impact of war on the children of veterans would have to wait another few decades after my sister's death. It took veterans coming home from another war, Vietnam, for researchers to look at the implications of a father's war trauma on his children. Finally, the National Center for the Study of PTSD (NCPTSD) was created in 1989 as part of the Veterans Administration's belated outreach to deal with PTSD, but even then, the focus was on the veterans of the Vietnam War. World War II and Korean War veterans were still not considered to be a population in need of mental health services.

The VA had established the Center to focus on research and education, with the seven divisions spread across the country from New England to Hawaii. While the awareness of a father's war trauma on his children has now become accepted in psychological literature, there has still been scant analysis of the effects of war trauma in the home of World War II veterans. In 1986, the only published study of post-traumatic stress disorder and children in World War II families was presented in the *Journal of Nervous Mental Disorders* by psychiatrist Robert Rosenheck. This extremely small sample of five families revealed that whether or not the children had a conscious knowledge of their father's combat experience, there was an evident trans-generational impact that continued into the adult lives of the children of these veterans.[3]

Subsequent research by NCPTSD and others continued to focus on the impact of Vietnam on families. The post-Vietnam analysis identified typical behavior patterns in children of combat veterans who had PTSD. Secondary traumatization, also known as compassion fatigue, may be

---

3. Robert Rosenheck, "Impact of posttraumatic stress disorder of World War II on the next generation," *Journal of Nervous and Mental Disease* 174 (1986), 319–27.

present in the children of the veterans and acted out in different scenarios. With secondary traumatization, the child picks up on the father's trauma and PTSD symptoms. A direct relationship has been found between the father's symptoms and the various behaviors of their children. An over-identified child shares nightmares and flashbacks with their Dads, who are the central focus of the child's energy. A rescuer or "parentified" child assumes the role of caretaker, absorbing guilt about the family problems and trying to be the fixer. An emotionally uninvolved child, on the surface, seems well-adjusted and performs well in school. With that coping mechanism, the child detaches from the family drama; they usually receive little emotional support and guidance from their parents. This high-performance surface appearance covers up the anxiety and depression that the child is internalizing, a symptom that my sister exhibited.[4]

The aftermath of Vietnam fostered more psychological studies with titles like "Secondary Traumatization in Children of Vietnam Veterans."[5] The generation of children raised by Vietnam veterans was well aware, through the media's lopsided presentation of the "troubled" Vietnam vet, that their fathers may have returned home changed men. The psychiatric community, having formalized the PTSD diagnosis in 1980, was now broadening its outlook to include family dynamics.

A memoir about the impact of a father's Vietnam war experience was a New York Times bestseller and chosen by the paper as one of the ten best books of 2006. *Falling through the Earth* by Danielle Trussoni is an evocative recounting of a daughter growing up with a combat-scarred father. Thirty years after his tour of duty ended, Danielle, his eldest daughter, explored why the boy who went off to war came back a battle-hardened alcoholic, eventually diagnosed with post-traumatic stress disorder.[6] It took much longer for children of World War II combat veterans to recognize the toll their fathers' war had taken on their psyches.

Not until *Saving Private Ryan* in 1998 did the reality of our fathers' war appear on the big screen. Until then, World War II movies were

---

4. Jennifer L. Price, Ph.D., "When a Child's Parent Has PTSD," National Center for PTSD, U.S. Dept. of Veterans Affairs, accessed August 5, 2011, http://www.ptsd.va.gov/professional/pages/pro_child_parent_ptsd.asp.

5. Robert Rosenheck & Pramila Nathan, "Secondary Traumatization in Children of Vietnam Veterans," Hospital and Community Psychiatry 36(5) (1985), 538–39.

6. Danielle Trussoni, *Falling Through the Earth: A Memoir* (New York: Henry Holt and Co., 2006).

mainly filmed in black and white with bloodless deaths. Chris Kalten-bach, a columnist for the *Baltimore Sun*, correctly noted that *Saving Private Ryan* was a World War II movie like none before. Hollywood had previously depicted the "good war" as a mythic and heroic undertaking. Kaltenbach calls *Private Ryan* the most graphic war film since *Platoon* and possibly the most graphic ever. People get shot and die hard, not quickly and quietly. Men's insides spill onto the ground as they watch, helpless. Civilized men are forced to do things barbarians would have hesitated doing."[7] Visual celluloid reality finally depicted our Dad's war in all its gory mess. For me, *The Longest Day* would no longer be my touchstone for the recreating of Dutch Schultz's battle experience.

At the end of the twentieth century, middle-aged children of World War II combat vets slowly began to walk out of the shadows with their stories, more than five decades after VE day. By exposing blood and guts and deromanticizing our fathers' war, Steven Spielberg, the son of a vet-eran of the Pacific Theater in World War II, unleashed the hidden turmoil of a generation. Gradually, children were telling their stories of the reality of living with a World War II combat vet, a tale that, in some cases, was a far cry from the image of the perfect Greatest Generation family.

The publication of *Flags of Our Fathers* told the truth about the iconic flag-raising at Iwo Jima. The author, James Bradley, is the son of one of the six military men in the famous photo. His father, John Bradley, was the Navy medic for the unit. Bradley was the only one of the six men who had a relatively well-adjusted postwar life, although he remained haunted for decades by his closest friend's brutal death on Iwo Jima. Three of the Marines in the picture soon died on that blood-spattered island. Two of the survivors, Ira Hayes and Rene Gagnon, never recovered from the trauma of the Pacific War. In 1955, Hayes died of exposure and alcohol poisoning; he collapsed into a ditch while in a drunken stupor. Gagnon died in the 1970s, an alcoholic, bitter and frustrated because none of the job opportunities offered to him when he was a "hero" ever materialized.[8]

Julia Collins, in *My Father's War*, outlined the corrosive effects of World War II on her father. Corporal Jerry Collins was a product of an

---

7. Chris Kallenbach, "Killing the war myth 'Saving Private Ryan' skips the romantic-hero routine and shows the field of combat in all its ugliness and horror." *The Baltimore Sun*, July 19, 1998.

8. James Bradley with Ron Powers, *Flags of Our Fathers* (New York: Bantam Books, 2000).

accelerated wartime program at Yale University when he went to war in 1943. He was a "lucky" Marine survivor of the brutal Pacific campaign against the Japanese. After his homecoming, he never again pursued his dream of becoming a chemist. Afflicted with survivor's guilt, he was haunted by grotesque memories of gory battles until his death. His family's well-being was affected by his chronic alcoholism, unemployment and psychological torment during the post-war years. This dark retrospective illustrates how Jerry Collins' promising future ended on the bloody islands of Okinawa and Guadalcanal. As a young child, the author was burdened with her troubled father's bloody bedtime stories told to her as she was drifting off to sleep.[9]

In a son's biting book, *Our Father's War: Growing Up in the Shadow of the Greatest Generation*, Tom Mathews wove his story together with the experiences of nine other sons of World War II veterans. These men all shared a common antagonism towards their Dads. They struggled with anger at their fathers' rigidity and macho expectations. Not until his adult years did Mathews directly relate the void between father and son to the emotional repression of horrific war experiences. This exploration of the trans-generational impact on Baby Boomer sons of hardened combat vets of World War II demonstrated how the hidden anguish of the fathers translated into fractured relationships with their sons.[10]

Thomas Childers, the noted historian at the University of Pennsylvania, son of a World War II veteran, and nephew to a B-24 radio operator who died on the last bomber shot down over Germany before VE day, uncovered the truth of postwar veteran experiences in his narrative *Soldier From the War Returning: The Greatest Generation's Troubled Homecoming From World War II*. Weaving compelling stories of three veterans with impeccable historical research, his work is an exploration of the darker side of World War II, a description of the physical and emotional turmoil experienced by the men and their families behind closed doors.[11]

A book by the daughter of a World War II Army doctor reveals how the unspoken, hidden horror of World War II can reverberate through a

9. Julia Collins, *My Father's War* (New York: Four Walls, Eight Windows, 2002).
10. Tom Mathews, *Our Father's War: Growing Up in the Shadow of the Greatest Generation* (New York: Broadway Books, 2005).
11. Thomas Childers, *Soldier from the War Returning: The Great Generation's Troubled Homecoming from World War II* (New York: Houghton Mifflin, 2009).

family. In *Gated Grief: The Daughter of a Concentration Camp Liberator Discovers a Legacy of Trauma*, Leila Levinson attempted to understand her own father's experience through her interviews with other veterans who came face to face with the Holocaust. Reuben Levinson's war story was unknown to his daughter until after his death, when she unearthed appalling photographs of Nordhausen, a sub-camp of Buchenwald, in a trunk that was stored in the basement of her father's medical office. She discovered that he had been in that concentration camp for two weeks, treating Holocaust survivors. She also learned that her father had an emotional breakdown after this and that his return home from war was delayed for months when the Army sent him to the Riviera for rest and relaxation.[12]

After decades of silence, the illusion of the perfect post-World War II happy family is being challenged by children who grew up in families that didn't fit the prevalent stereotype. But the illusion dies hard. An April 30, 2009, post on *The Art of Manliness* is indicative of that. Using Brokaw's book as evidence of how World War II veterans were manlier, the blog's authors offer life lessons from the Greatest Generation, including the following:

Lesson #4: Love Loyally
The men of the *Greatest Generation* took their marriage vows seriously. Brokaw wrote, "It was the last generation in which, broadly speaking, marriage was a commitment and divorce was not an option. I can't remember one of my parents' friends who were divorced. In the communities where we lived, it was treated as a minor scandal." The numbers bear Brokaw's anecdotal evidence out: of all the new marriages in 1940, 1 in 6 ended in divorce. By the late 1990s, that number was 1 in 2.[13]

These numbers are skewed—1940 was a year before the beginning of World War II, but the statistic is presented to demonstrate the belief

12. Leila Levinson, *Gated Grief: The Daughter of a Concentration Camp Liberator Discovers a Legacy of Trauma* (Brule, Wisconsin: Cable Publishing, 2011).

13. Brett & Kate McKay, "7 Lessons in Manliness from the Greatest Generation," The Art of Manliness, http://artofmanliness.com/2009/04/30/7—lessons -in-manliness-from-the-greatest-generation/, accessed April 14, 2010.

that marriages and families were untroubled after World War II. The reality is that one year after the end of the war in 1946, the divorce rate was at an all-time high of 4.6. That rate was not equaled again until the mid-1970s.

Children like my sister Rosemary and me, who didn't realize that their fathers' war had had a major impact on their families, will never be counted as among the "collateral" damage of World War II, and the truth of what the Greatest Generation's combat veterans brought back from war will never be adequately measured. There is no reverse time machine, no applying today's knowledge to the past. Still, the recognition that World War II families fought similar battles on the home front will eliminate the isolation of veterans' children from the oft-titled "good war." It will hopefully stand as a cautionary tale to give military children of today's wars attention and support when their fathers' war comes home to stay.

Rosemary Schultz graduation, 1969.

Rosemary Schultz, 1970.

6

FROM MANURE TO MAHOGANY

*By 1942, the cruiser had become the principal surface combat ship
in the Pacific. In addition to screening the fast carrier attack forces,
cruisers carried out gunnery raids on enemy-held shores, provided fire
support for amphibious operations, and were given many assignments
in support of general fleet operations. From her original role as a
scout and surface raider, the cruiser became an essential component
of task force operations in the Pacific. During the war, the United
States completed large numbers of cruisers to meet the demands of
fleet operations in the Pacific. These ships continued to bear the brunt
of the action in the Pacific until the end of the war.*

—National Park Service, World War II Warships in the Pacific

Two World War II veterans have had an abiding influence on my life.
During my early years, Dutch was a role model for persistence in the face
of overwhelming odds. Despite our familial turmoil, my Dad and I had
an unshakeable bond until he died in 2005.

My stepfather, Lee Bondy, entered my life in my adult years and
has filled a fatherly role, anchoring and steady. He is the prototypical
Greatest Generation figure, embodying the life path and traits society
identified as characteristic of that cadre of men. His educational achieve-
ments and successful business career, in all likelihood, were fueled by his
participation in World War II.[1]

Born in Stillwater, Minnesota, in 1925 to a second-generation Nor-
wegian father and a Dutch mother, Lee's formative years were spent in
a nomadic fashion. He often lived with extended family and performed
chores on their various farms and ranches. When his parents divorced in

---

1. *Lee Bondy, From Manure to Mahogany: Memoirs of a Depression Child* (Booklocker.com, 2007). All
the material in this chapter about Lee Bondy is from this source.

1933, the judge gave each of the three Bondy children a choice of the parental home. Lee, the middle child, picked his father, Melvin, mainly because he stood alone and desolate in the courtroom. The eldest son, Roger, and daughter, Phyllis, had chosen to live with their mother. Thus began Lee's exposure to tough conditions in the Upper Midwest. Melvin's brother, Knute Konow Bondy, was a homesteader in Richland, an isolated area in the northeastern quadrant of Montana bordering North Dakota. Knute's thousand-acre ranch teemed with horses, milk cows, chickens, turkeys, pigs, prairie dogs and fields of wheat. Lee was often left with Uncle Knute, his wife and their thirteen children, while Dad Melvin worked at a local bar/restaurant in town. Living conditions during the nineteen thirties on the Great Plains were archaic compared to city comforts. Winters were bone-chilling and rugged, and summer days were filled with chores. Crop failure was all too common. Plagues of locusts swarmed for miles over fields, ruining the harvest, and the infamous drought of the nineteen thirties, which caused the "Dust Bowl," also reached into Montana. Green cutworms were yet another nuisance, covering the fields like a giant moving green sheet and eating all the wheat or other vegetation in its path.

The Montana ranch house did not offer electricity, indoor plumbing, or enough sleeping room for all the children. Girls slept in the main house, while boys were relegated to the bunkhouse, heated by one potbellied stove that burned dried cow manure. Winters were definitely a challenge. The boys woke up to frost on their bedding and jumped into their overalls, frozen rigid from moisture left from the sweat of the previous day. Bathing occurred weekly. An oversized laundry tub was filled with water boiled in the main house. The order of bathing in the bunkhouse was according to age. Since Lee was the youngest, by the time it was his turn, lukewarm and dirty water awaited him. The boys seldom stayed in the main house—only to eat their meals and listen to the battery-operated, vacuum tube radio.

Milking cows, manure spreading, and castrating bulls were some of the skills young Lee learned during the Depression years. He could name every breed of cow, horse, chicken, and pig and also hold forth on the value of crop rotation. His formal education took place in a one-room schoolhouse ten miles from the ranch. Horseback was the only means of transportation, and Lee never missed a day. All school grades were taught together by an itinerant teacher who had been sent to the rural school for student teaching experience. Lee benefited from being in the room with older students and exposure to advanced material. A natural in math, by the sixth grade, he was testing way above grade level. His intelligence was obvious, and by eighth grade, when most of his peers had completed their education, his teacher recommended that he attend high school in Peerless, Montana. He boarded in the town for high school. His expenses were covered by uncle Knute's monthly offering of a freshly butchered cow or pig.

After two years at school in Peerless, Lee was on the move again. He moved in with another one of Melvin's brothers, Iver Bondy, in Bemidji, Minnesota. This town was the home of the statue of Paul Bunyan and Babe, his Blue Ox, which have been on the National Register of Historic Places since 1988. These massive structures first appeared in Bemidji during their winter carnival of 1937, a public relations move designed to bring notice to the town as a venue for winter sports. Bemidji has also been called the "curling capital" of America. With extremely cold temperatures in the winter, often hovering twenty to thirty degrees below zero, the Scottish ice game took hold in the town during the 1930s. Curling did not appeal to Lee. He preferred ice fishing. With wooden decoys, he would spear unsuspecting fish and bring them home for dinner.

During the first few years of the 1940s, high school seemed indeterminable to Lee. Even though he excelled at academics, science and math in particular, he was worried that World War II would be over before he was old enough to enlist. Finally, after high school graduation in 1943, he attempted to enlist at the Navy Recruiting station, only to be rejected three times for poor eyesight. However, by the end of the summer of 1943, Lee received his draft notice and was slated to enter the Army. After he reported to Fort Snelling, Minnesota, he took a number of aptitude tests. His score was so high that he was offered his choice of Army Officer Candidate School or Navy electronic training school. Finally accepted by his first choice, the Navy, he was sent to basic training at the Farragut Naval Base, situated inland in northwestern Idaho, far away from America's West Coast and the possibility of a Japanese attack. Between the opening of the base in September 1942 and its decommissioning in June 1946, this stunning expanse of 4,000 acres at Farragut served as a temporary home to almost 300,000 naval recruits. The base briefly became Idaho's largest city during World War II. During training, Navy recruits, many of them away from home for the first time, came to Farragut and learned how to march, row, swim and use firearms before heading off to the Mediterranean Sea or the Pacific.

After Farragut, Lee was sent for more advanced training in electronics, sonar, and radar at installations in the Great Lakes area and Treasure Island in San Francisco. After a year of this intensive training, he became an ETR-2 (Electronic Technician Radar) and was sent to Naval medical testing to determine his physical fitness. This exam would determine whether Lee would be a landlubber or a shipboard sailor. Increasingly worried that the eye examination would disqualify him for overseas duty, he memorized the responses of ten recruits ahead of him in line. Not only did he pass, but he was also rated as having twenty-twenty vision. After he faked the exam, he was assigned for duty on a light cruiser in the Pacific Theater, the USS *Cleveland*. The ship had finished its first tour of duty in late 1944 and had seen a great deal of action, providing support for major battles in the Pacific, including Morocco, North Africa, New Caledonia, Guadalcanal, Bougainville, Green Island, Guam and Peleliu.

Prior to the *Cleveland*'s second tour, the ship returned to the States and anchored at Terminal Island in San Pedro, California, to be overhauled. The ship, nicknamed "Charlie Charlie Love Five," was outfitted with the newest radar and fire control equipment. Weapons were updated, and the heavy machine gun battery was doubled. The veteran crew was joined by two hundred new men, Lee among them. As the only ship technician aboard, Lee was responsible for maintaining the radar system. He was on call twenty-four hours a day, grabbing sleep whenever he had a spare moment. *Cleveland*'s radar provided a capability for long-range interception of enemy planes, with five-inch anti-aircraft guns and autocannons responding quickly to bring down Japanese kamikaze planes. Lee was involved in his first major naval battle in mid-February 1945 when the fight to recapture the Philippine Islands started with cruisers, destroyers and aerial bombardment. The Allies had endured a bloody exit from the island in the spring of 1942, and the aftermath of that ignominious defeat had brought harsh and inhumane treatment to captured

Allied troops. Seventy-five thousand American and Filipino prisoners were forcibly marched sixty miles by their Japanese captors to an internment camp. On this brutal Bataan Death March, thousands died from torture, beatings, and a lack of food and water. The surviving prisoners were transported to Japan on "Hell Ships" and trucked to horrid prisoner-of-war camps to be used as labor for the Japanese war machine.

The key to recapturing the Philippines began with the battle for Corregidor, which involved a two-pronged, airborne and amphibious attack by the Allies. The *Cleveland*, along with the rest of the naval fleet, shelled the island to soften up the area prior to the jump of one thousand paratroopers from the 503rd Regimental Combat Team and the simultaneous beach landing of the Third Battalion of the 24th Infantry Division on San Jose Point. Fierce battles raged for days. Enemy defenders holed up in caves and tunnels and attempted unsuccessfully to waylay the American troops. Finally, the island was secured by the Americans by the end of February 1945. Some remaining Japanese soldiers blew themselves up in tunnels and caves rather than surrendering to American forces.

Fulfilling the promise he had made in 1942, General Douglas MacArthur triumphantly returned on March 7, 1945, to Manila Harbor, almost three years after his defeat in the Philippines in April 1942. After the *Cleveland* patrolled the Philippine Islands for a few months, the ship was dispatched to Subic Bay in British North Borneo. The cruiser was part of a covering force, which provided fire support for invasion landings by Australian troops on June 10, 1945, at Balikpapan, Brunei Bay. A few weeks after that action, the ship was chosen, because of its speed and firepower, to pick up General Douglas MacArthur from Manila and bring him to Balikpapan to observe. He disembarked from the *Cleveland* and made an inspection tour of the landing area at Borneo. Always mindful of public relations, the General waded ashore with great fanfare, accompanied by a bevy of photographers and reporters, and remained on shore for three hours before he was hurried back to Manila. For their role in transporting him, Lee and the rest of the crew were given eight by ten glossy photos of the General.

The *Cleveland* readied for its next stop, Okinawa, and arrived there on July 16, 1945. It did not encounter any Japanese ships during late July and August, but enemy planes were always a constant threat. Kamikaze attacks were ongoing. Lee was on constant call. Radar had to function perfectly so that the ship's guns could down the planes. Finally, on August 12, 1945, the *Cleveland* received word that Japan had requested terms of surrender, a few days after atomic bombs had been dropped on Hiroshima and Nagasaki. Lee remembers troops on the beach firing rockets into the air. Crews on the ships screamed and shouted with joy. In the midst of the celebration and festivities, a new wave of kamikaze planes arrived, strafed the fleet, and sunk the USS *Pennsylvania* anchored next to the *Cleveland*. A Japanese torpedo plane had slipped in over Buckner Bay without detection and launched a torpedo at the *Pennsylvania*. The ship suffered extensive damage and flooding. Twenty crew members were killed, and ten were injured, including Admiral Oldendorf, who broke several ribs. The *Cleveland* and the other ships in the fleet were ordered out to sea. The Navy feared that the surrender talks were a ruse. Finally, on August 15, 1945, the war ended. Emperor Hirohito announced that Japan would comply with the terms of the Potsdam Declaration. The formal ceremony of surrender took place on the USS *Missouri* in Tokyo Bay on September 2, 1945.

By September 9, 1945, Lee and the rest of the *Cleveland* crew were ordered to take positions around the Japanese mainland to ensure that a peaceful post-surrender ensued. On the way to Japan, they encountered a fierce typhoon near Okinawa. Many smaller vessels were swamped, but Lee's ship stayed afloat, albeit with fifty-foot waves causing it to bob like a cork. After the storm subsided, the ship made its way to Wakayama, dropping anchor on September 15, 1945. The *Cleveland* covered the evacuation of Allied prisoners of war onto hospital ships. It also sent advance invasion parties ashore to confirm that there was no resistance from the population. Lee noticed that there were no women to be seen on the mainland. The Japanese government had warned women that they would be targets of rape and assault by American troops.

After occupation duties were over, the *Cleveland* sailed to Hawaii. Acting under orders, Lee threw all the radar equipment overboard, as it was now considered surplus. He then had a few days of R&R in Hawaii. He lacked sufficient points for discharge, so he was reassigned to Key West, Florida, on a ship that had similar radar equipment to the *Cleveland*. Finally, in June 1946, Lee completed his military obligation. He returned home with Bronze Stars and a Combat Action Ribbon and was demobilized at Fort Snelling, Minnesota, a civilian once again.

Lee hoped to build on the training and experience that the Navy had given him, and upon homecoming, he enrolled in college. Taking advantage of the GI Bill, Lee enrolled first at Bemidji State Teachers College, with the understanding that the credits were transferable to the University of Minnesota. The war had given him the opportunity to expand his horizons; he was the only member of his extended family to attend college. The skills he had learned during the war years were transferable to civilian life. Once he received his electrical engineering degree in 1950, he was primed to enter the professional workforce, but war again interfered since Lee was still in the Naval Reserves. This time, during the Korean War, his duty was a lot less combative. He was stationed in Hawaii and lived in Waikiki Beach while teaching radar and sonar classes for recruits. After Lee's honorable discharge in June 1952, his long-awaited entry into the business world began.

Douglas Aircraft in Long Beach, California, was his first stop. Lee's initial job was to assist in the development of the DC-8, the company's first jet-powered airliner. During his time at Douglas, Lee became proficient in the development of aircraft sensors. This ability led to his involvement with Schaevitz Engineering Company, a premier sensor producer, first as General Manager and then as company President for many years. He ended his long and illustrious career when he was nearing eighty, as President of another company, MacroSensors, a leading designer and manufacturer of sensors utilized in industrial and aerospace companies.

If not for World War II and the training and experience that Lee received fighting the Japanese on that Navy cruiser, he might have never left the ranching/farming life and would have spent his life presiding over a domain of cows, horses, pigs and wheat. Lee learned a skill during his war years. The existence of the GI Bill aided him in achieving a middle-class status that he may never have known otherwise. Fifty-two weeks of unemployment assistance, medical assistance, and a guaranteed four years of education placed Lee Bondy on a life path that otherwise may have been out of reach.

My stepdad's transition into civilian life was different from my father's rocky re-entry. Lee exemplified the prototypical Greatest Generation trajectory upward. Many combat veterans, upon their return home, did not have a transferable skill. Spencer Wurst, an 82nd Airborne veteran of four combat jumps, articulated high levels of frustration in his book *Descending From the Clouds,* describing the exit interview he had with an Army captain when he was demobilized. The captain's potpourri of decorations did not include any evidence of overseas or combat action. The captain persistently asked Spencer: "What did you really do in the war? What skills did you learn?"

Lieutenant Wurst, getting angry and agitated, replied, "You don't have to put anything on that form . . . because there's not much need in civilian life for how to throw a grenade, push a bayonet into someone, shoot people, tear down a machine gun and reassemble it."

Wurst said that he and his buddies on the front lines anticipated that when it came to getting a job in the civilian world, those who saw the most combat would be disadvantaged while veterans in support positions who had learned a trade would be able to capitalize on that training after the war.[2]

There is no question that the Greatest Generation moniker is deserved. The narrative, however, has been distorted. By the lack of understanding and acknowledgment of the experiences of veterans whose war experiences consisted mainly of bloodshed in combat, we diminish their contributions and ignore their suffering. Comparing my father's and my stepfather's war experiences illustrates that each soldier, sailor, or marine had a different story. The sanitization of their stories into one overarching storyline has deluded us into viewing the World War II veterans through a monochromatic lens, devoid of individuality.

Both my father and my stepfather contributed mightily to the war effort. Both served their country with distinction. Both were involved in combat. However, one returned scarred, while the other used the expertise he developed throughout his war years as a springboard for further education and an extremely successful business career. Both were in combat zones. The difference was one of degree and duration. Whether dropped from the sky as in Normandy or marched on the ground into the Bulge, paratroopers fought battles as a strike force, first into the fight.

---

2. Spencer F. Wurst & Gayle Wurst, *Descending from the Clouds: A Memoir of Combat in the 505 Parachute Infantry Regiment, 82nd Airborne Division* (Drexel Hill, PA: Casemate, 2007), 256.

Heavy combat exposure has been shown to affect long-term mental and physical health. Physical decline and premature death have impacted those World War II veterans who were continually in battle. Intense combat exposure influenced the likelihood and severity of PTSD in World War II veterans, a finding that is of significance to researchers but not a concern, except to the family members who are often on the front lines with their veteran, who are hostages to the never-ending flashbacks and nightmares, emotional numbing, and survivor's guilt.[3]

Mental health issues of Vietnam veterans have been a topic of academic interest and compassionate societal concern for years; however, there has been scant follow-up on the psychological health of World War II combat veterans. The cookie-cutter approach, stereotyping the Greatest Generation as a unified mass of men who came marching home to build America into a superpower, is inadequate. Gerald Linderman, in *The World Within War: America's Combat Experience in World War II*, described the returning combat veteran as someone struggling with his battle memories, using repression to cover his private anguish, which the American public ignored and denied, and the collective societal memory of the war, almost eight decades after its end, still reflects this denial.[4]

---

3. Glen H. Elder, Michael J. Shanahan, Elizabeth C. Clipp, "The Legacy of World War II in Men's Lives," *American Journal of Psychiatry*, 154:3 (1997), 330–36. See also: K.A. Lee, G.E. Torrey, G.H. Elder, "A 50-year prospective study of the psychological sequelae of World War II combat," *American Journal of Psychiatry*, 152:4 (1995), 516–22.

4. Gerald Linderman, *The World Within War: American Combat Experience in World War II* (New York: Free Press, 1997), 359, 361.

Lee Bondy, 1944.

Mom and Lee.

7

WARRIORS' UNEASY RETURN

The veteran has psychoneurosis, chronic anxiety reaction, extreme tenseness and self-pity with a low tolerance for frustration, inability to digest wartime experiences, recurrent depressive episodes with secondary alcoholism, and marginal social and poor economic and occupational adjustment. Marked Impairment.

Veterans Administration file – Psychiatric Evaluation

This diagnosis of a patient seen by a VA psychiatrist in San Diego reads like a classic description of a traumatized Vietnam veteran. Jonathan Shay has been lauded for his book *Achilles in Vietnam*, which provides the American public with an overview of the aftereffects of combat in soldiers returning from the Vietnam War. The image of troubled Baby Boomer warriors, plagued by substance abuse and psychological problems, has been paired with the representation of an ungrateful nation, which greeted them with hostility upon homecoming.[1] This paradigm stands in sharp contrast to the warm welcome given to World War II combatants. Emblazoned in our consciousness are idyllic scenes of parades with crowds of people cheering and waving flags, welcoming home their heroes. According to Shay's comparison of homecomings from the two different wars, the long ride across the ocean was supposedly the main difference that enabled our World War II boys to support each other in digesting their wartime experiences.[2]

Tom Brokaw has further perpetuated the commonly accepted view of the Greatest Generation's uncomplicated homecoming. Brokaw coined the phrase of tribute in *The Greatest Generation*, the first in his series of books extolling the virtues of the heroes of World War II.

1. Jonathan Shay, *Achilles in Vietnam: Combat Trauma and the Undoing of Character* (New York: Simon & Schuster, 1995), 8.
2. Shay, 61.

They succeeded on every front. They won the war; they saved
the world. They came home to joyous and short-lived celebra-
tions and immediately began the task of rebuilding their lives
and the world they wanted. They married in record numbers
and gave birth to another distinctive generation, the Baby
Boomers.[3]

Certainly, these men were indeed heroes, but the prevalent generational snapshot is a one-sided, incomplete recounting, reliant on impression and cultural myth for what it lacks in historical fact. The psychiatric
evaluation presented at the start of this chapter is not a description of a
Vietnam veteran; rather, it is taken from the Veterans Administration
file on my father, the hard-bitten combat paratrooper. Written nineteen
years after the hostilities of World War II ended, it demonstrates how one
man's battle with the war never ended for him.[4] Moreover, it complicates
the narrative of the "Good War." Because of the huge disparity between
what we were experiencing in our families and what we saw in the media,
many of us who had World War II combat fathers felt a dissonance with
the widely accepted view and searched for the flaw that prevented our
families from living the post-war American dream.

Society's refusal to recognize the turmoil and trauma suffered by the
combat veteran of World War II spurred me to investigate the history
and social science regarding the experience of veterans like my father,
brave men who endured and survived much. What I discovered was a
complete lack of research on World War II combat veterans, as well as
an incorrect view of their experience. For example, the supposition that
post-traumatic stress disorder began with the Vietnam veteran is pervasive, partly due to the male ethos of emotional stoicism of the World War
II vet, but also because historical facts concerning World War II soldiers
have been superseded by mythology, which is not always accurate.

Another common misperception about World War II soldiers is that
there was little psychological trauma upon their return because of strong

---

3. Tom Brokaw, *The Greatest Generation* (New York: Random House, 1998), book jacket, inside front
flap.
4. Arthur Schultz, neuropsychiatric examination, Veterans Administration file of Arthur Schultz,
1946–2005.

troop cohesion—men went over to battle together on foreign soil and came back as a unit with their brothers in arms at the end of the war. In reality, except for the beginning days of the war, a soldier was assigned to a unit as an individual. After training, he was sent to a repple depple (replacement depot), from which he was assigned to a unit that had been in combat and had taken casualties. For the most part, replacements were ignored by the old-timers.[5] Why bother, they thought? Newcomers did not have combat experience and were likely to be killed or wounded. Waiting to jump out of a C-47 into Normandy, my Dad was one of those fresh replacements, nervously fingering his rosary on the bumpy trip over the English Channel. In Dad's history written for Stephen Ambrose's *D-Day* book, my father recounted,

> I looked around and saw a number of the old timers sleeping and catching catnaps . . . There was a lot of rocking and rolling. And I remember looking out the window, and I thought I saw sparks coming out of one of the engines, and I turned to one of these veterans . . . and I said, 'Look at those sparks coming out of the engines.' And he looked at me and said, 'Sparks, hell. That's flak. That's Ack-Ack.' And that was the first awareness I had that things weren't going to be merely like a practice jump.[6]

This replacement method of plugging in individual soldiers for combat positions wherever they were needed certainly undermined unit cohesion. According to Wikipedia, the depots were found to be ineffective, as men assigned from these large pools had poor esprit de corps. Soldiers seldom went to a unit with the men with whom they had trained, and they were often unfamiliar with the fighting formations to which they were subsequently assigned. The handling of replacements in this bulk, impersonal way tended to cause psychological trauma because the soldiers felt unprepared, frightened, and isolated.[7]

---

5. Rich Anderson, "U.S. Army in World War II: Manpower and Segregation," *Military History Online*, accessed August 10, 2011, http://www.militaryhistoryonline.com/wwii/usarmy/manpower.aspx.

6. Stephen Ambrose, "Schultz—D-Day," Kalikow Collection, National World War II Museum, New Orleans, LA, 4.

7. "Replacement Depot," *Wikipedia*, accessed August 10, 2011, en.Wikipedia.org/wiki/Replacement depot.

At the end of the war, soldiers were once again cut off from their buddies. World War II was the first war in which points determined the release from service date. Therefore, demobilization occurred individually rather than by unit. Under the point system, the serviceman's return home was based on having a total of 85 points. Points were accumulated by the length of time in service, length of time overseas, combat experience, combat awards and dependent children. The World War II combatant with the most exposure to death and destruction was likely to be one of the first to return home, not necessarily surrounded by his battle buddies but on a ship with others who may not have been in his unit.[8]

The idea of an unencumbered homecoming for the World War II veteran also rests on the assumption that there were few psychiatric wounds in the "good war's" victorious soldiers, in contrast to veterans who returned after the loss in Vietnam, but research has demonstrated that there have been psychiatric wounds after every American war. In Eric Dean's book, *Shook Over Hell: Post-Traumatic Stress, Vietnam, and the Civil War,* the author notes that even though the terms used to describe the condition of post-traumatic stress were different, the symptoms were the same.[9] After the Civil War, even Union veterans were categorized as suffering from nostalgia, insanity, soldiers' or irritable hearts. Many came home from World War I with shell shock, a term descriptive of the reaction to a shell explosion, which was thought to cause nervousness and anxiety in the men exposed.[10]

Spurred by the experience of World War I, whereby it was thought that emotional weakness in a soldier predisposed him to shell shock, policymakers were already making plans in 1940, prior to the outbreak of World War II, to weed out the weak.[11] Based on a plan created by a psychoanalyst, Henry Stack Sullivan, for the Selective Service System in 1940, the program required psychiatric screenings for the young men who would be fighting in World War II. More than a million and a half men were found to be "mentally unfit" and disqualified from service. This rate was more than six times the rejection rate for World War I.

---

8. James Ciment, Thadeus Russell, eds., *The Home Front Encyclopedia: United States, Britain, and Canada in World Wars I and II* (Santa Barbara, CA: ABC-CLIO, 2007), 834.

9. Eric T. Dean, *Shook Over Hell: Post-Traumatic Stress, Vietnam and the Civil War* (Cambridge, MA: Harvard University Press, 1997), 129–31.

10. Dean, 31.

11. Dean, 35.

These initial screenings were supposed to eliminate soldier collapse. As a result, combat fatigue was not taken seriously during the early years of the war.[12] A soldier who broke down emotionally was given the bare minimum of care in a battlefield hospital. Military leaders were unprepared for the large number of men who suffered from war neurosis; estimates are double the number in World War I. Finally, in 1943, General Omar Bradley, commander of the 12th Army Group in Europe, required a seven-day holding period for a soldier diagnosed with psychiatric exhaustion.[13] On May 24th, 1943, Time Magazine gave news coverage to an American Psychiatric Association meeting in which the Commander of a Naval Hospital in California described the new disorder, "Guadalcanal Neurosis." Commander Edwin Smith described "a group neurosis" that occurred after prolonged warfare on Guadalcanal. He had treated over five hundred Marines from that killing island and described their physical and mental strain as combining the "best of Edgar Allan Poe and Buck Rogers . . . Rain, heat, insects, dysentery, malaria all contributed—but the result was not bloodstream infection nor gastrointestinal disease, but a disturbance of the whole organism, a disorder of thinking and living, of even wanting to live." The symptoms displayed by these hard-bitten Marines included "headaches, sensitivity to sharp noises, periods of amnesia, a tendency to get panicky, tense muscles, tremors, hands that shook when they tried to do anything. They were 'frequently close to tears or very short-tempered.'" Commander Smith felt that it was doubtful these men could go back to the type of combat that they had been exposed to on Guadalcanal.[14]

With the evidence that elite troops like Marines were susceptible to combat exhaustion, military thinking changed from over-reliance on screening to an understanding that every man had a breaking point. Screening for mental defects before enlistment was abolished by General George Marshall in 1944 since the process had not reduced the incidence of nervous exhaustion among World War II warriors.[15]

12. David H. Marlowe, *Psychological and Psychosocial Consequences of Combat with Special Emphasis on the Gulf War* (Santa Monica, CA: Rand, 2001), Chapter 7.

13. Franklin D. Jones, Linetter Sparacano, Victoria Wilcox, Joseph Rothberg, James Stokes, *War Psychiatry* (Bethesda, MD: Uniformed Services University of the Health Sciences, 1995), 26.

14. "Medicine: Guadalcanal Neurosis," *Time Magazine*, May 24, 1943, accessed August 10, 2011, http://www.time.com/time/magazine/article/ 019171.933048.00.html.

15. Hans Pols and Stephanie Oak, "War and Military Mental Health," *American Journal of Public Health* 97(12) (December 2007), 2132–134.

Regardless of the awareness of the breaking point of a combat soldier, many with combat fatigue were sent back to the front lines unless they were nonfunctional. The more severe cases were taken out of action and often discharged. Almost half of medical discharges during World War II were for psychiatric reasons, the common diagnoses being psychoneurotic disorder or personality defects.

An accurate number of just how many soldiers returned home after the war with invisible wounds is not available. Post-traumatic stress disorder did not exist in 1945; it was not an official diagnosis in the *Diagnostic and Statistical Manual of Mental Disorders* (DSM) until the third edition in 1980.[16] In the 1940s, the assumption was that once a soldier was removed from combat, his trauma would disappear. A "tooth-to-tail ratio" in World War II was approximately one to four (combat troops including combat support) who were in combat zones, the remainder three quarters being support troops. Therefore, it is likely that four million of the sixteen million men who fought in World War II were exposed to combat conditions.[17] However, there is no way to determine retrospectively what percentage continued to suffer from war trauma upon homecoming. According to Dr. Matthew Friedman, Director of the VA's National Center for Post-traumatic Stress, the World War II veteran was rarely studied in terms of his psychological functioning after the war.[18]

Many of the veterans assuaged their unrecognized psychic turmoil with booze. Post-war alcoholism was a serious but poorly documented problem. Blame for problem drinking fell on the individual rather than the horrors of war, as a prevalent psychoanalytic theory of the day claimed that alcoholism was due to a personal flaw. Addictions like alcoholism were thought to be due to a character disorder, a failure of a "war ego" to transform into a "peace ego."[19]

Freudian theory dismissed combat as an independent source of trauma, claiming feelings of infantile anxiety and hostility had been repressed

---

16. Wilbur J. Scott, "PTSD in DSM-III: A Case in the Politics of Diagnosis and Disease," *Social Problems* 37(3) (August 1990), 234.

17. John C. McManus, *The Deadly Brotherhood: The American Combat Soldier in World War II* (Novato, CA: Presidio, 1998), 319.

18. Matthew Friedman, Ph.D., J.D. phone interview with author, May 24, 2007.

19. Ernst Simmel, M.D., "Alcoholism and Addiction," *Psychoanalytic Quarterly* 17 (1948), 6-31; See also, Louis Mesard and William F. Page, *Alcoholism and Problem Drinking 1970-1975: A Statistical Analysis of VA Hospital Patients* (Washington, D.C.: Veterans Administration, 1977).

in the soldier until his neurosis was aroused by war. In an analysis at a California Naval Hospital evaluating four combat veterans with outstanding records, the hospital's commander opined that their psychiatric problems and combat nightmares were symptomatic of underlying old neurosis. In spite of the fact that they were asymptomatic prior to the war, the veterans' troubles did not warrant a separate diagnosis connected with the war.[20]

The pervasiveness of blaming the individual for psychological issues is further demonstrated in the evaluation my father received in another futile attempt to receive help for his war trauma in 1957—his problems were classified as an anxiety reaction from an underlying "lifelong" character disorder. It didn't matter that he had never been previously diagnosed with a character disorder. Thanks to Freud, the assumption was that he would not have had anxiety if he had not been suffering from the character disorder all his life. Dad's symptoms in those years fit the profile presented in a 1945 book, *Men Under Stress in and after Combat*, written by Army Air Force officers, which was representative of the psychological literature of the forties and fifties. The men who were studied for this book spoke of "combat fear and other neurotic disturbances." In addition, these men were "ghosted by lost comrades"—a phenomenon which today would be considered a flashback.[21]

Men like my father and others with combat trauma who could still function may have been the lucky ones. While many psychological wounds were ignored or dismissed by the Veterans Administration, veterans who had mental and behavioral problems that were severe enough were often hospitalized and faced a variety of treatment options, all of which were grim. In the early 1950s, the VA system had a hundred and nine general hospitals and thirty-eight neuropsychiatric hospitals to deal with the institutionalized men, and more than half of the beds were filled with psychiatric cases, accounting for sixty percent of the veterans' hospitalizations in the 1950s.[22]

---

20. Samuel P. Hunt, "Analysis of Neurosis Developing After Combat in Four Individuals with Outstanding Combat Records," *Psychosomatic Medicine* 8 (1946), 258–70.

21. Ray Grinker and John Spiegel, *Men Under Stress in and after Combat* (Philadelphia, PA: The Blakiston Company, 1945), Introduction.

22. Wade E. Pickren, "VA Psychologists and Clinical Science in the 1950s," APA Online –Psychological Service Agenda, accessed August 10, 2011, http://www.apa.org.science/psa/novhistprint.html.

Two commonly used therapies in VA hospitals during those years were shock treatments: insulin or electric shock. Inducing insulin shock involved injecting patients with large doses of insulin for weeks. Daily comas, which supposedly would "shock" the patient's system out of mental illness, resulted from the insulin overdose. Electric shock operated on a similar principle of disordering the mind and jolting the veteran out of his mental distress. Electrodes were placed on the head of an anesthetized patient, sending an electric current to the brain, which caused the patient to seize[23] violently. In 1949, *The American Journal of Psychiatry* evaluated the effectiveness of shock treatments on one thousand veterans hospitalized for neuropsychiatric problems. These men received either insulin, electric shock, or both. The authors of the study noted, "the large percentage of social recoveries obtained in this group testifies amply to the efficacy of the shock therapies in the treatment of functional psychotic reactions incurred in wartime."[24] No mention was made of the disturbing side effects of the treatments. Insulin shock could cause brain damage and death, but to the Veterans Administration, it was considered effective because the procedure controlled problem patients. In 1951, eight patients who had been classified schizophrenic were studied after being put into protracted insulin comas at a New Jersey Veterans Hospital. The therapy was considered successful; the patients were deemed improved because of lessened tension and hostility, even though their delusions returned and their supposed improvement was preceded by "severe organic brain deficit." Electroshock also had complications, such as cognitive and memory deficits and compression fractures.[25]

Unfortunately, shock treatments were not the most egregious of the remedies used on World War II veterans treated for psychiatric problems in the VA system. Lobotomy, or psychosurgery, which consisted of severing the frontal lobes of the brain, was utilized to relieve anxiety and psychic distress. Research on the lobotomies performed on the

23. "A History of Somatic Therapies," MIRECC –Mind View Newsletter Archive, accessed August 10, 2011, http://www.desertpacific.mirecc.va.gov/mindview-archive/History-of-Somatic-Therapies-ar.

24. Samuel Paster and Saul C. Holtzman, "A Study of One Thousand Psychotic Veterans Treated with Insulin and Electric Shock," *American Journal of Psychiatry* 105 (May 1949), 811–14.

25. Eugene Revitch, "Observations on Organic Brain Damage and Chemical Improvement Following Protracted Insulin Coma," *Psychiatric Quarterly* 28(1), DOI:10.1007.BFO1567038. See also Barbara Young, "Vignettes from Psychiatric Training 1945–1951," *Perspectives in Biology and Medicine* 47(2) (Spring 2004), 227–43.

institutionalized veteran population in the 1950s was common, facilitated by a cooperative study process sponsored by the Veterans Administration. Using this model, VA hospitals that wished to be included in a particular study design were added; research subjects were taken from the hospitalized veteran population.[26] Accurate numbers regarding veterans who were lobotomized have never been released. While there is no exhaustive list, studies have been published about lobotomized patients at veterans' hospitals in Northport, New York; St. Cloud, Minnesota; Palo Alto, California; Lyons, New Jersey; Salem, Virginia; Perry Point, Virginia; and Tuskegee, Alabama.[27] The Tuskegee study specifically focused on African American lobotomized war veterans. Those patients who had been diagnosed with benign psychoneurotic problems, such as obsessive-compulsive disorder or hypochondria, along with manic depressives and schizophrenics, all had their frontal lobes severed in the name of research.[28] The use of lobotomy on the veteran population was at its highest point in the ten years following World War II and only began to diminish with the advent of pharmaceuticals for the treatment of mental illness. A retrospective study conducted in the 1960s by an associate chief of staff at a New Jersey veteran's hospital evaluated the success of lobotomies performed in the prior ten years. Patients who were given lobotomies had met the criteria of severe emotional tension, unmanageable assaultiveness, suicidal behavior, and failure to respond to shock therapies. According to the evaluator, the results were equivocal. Assaultiveness may have decreased, but over half the patients had post-lobotomy seizures, a quarter had significant intellectual disabilities,

---

26. Pickren, APA Online.

27. The following are studies relevant to World War II veterans lobotomized at Veterans Administration Hospitals: Lester Drubin, "Further Observations on Sixty-Two Lobotomized Psychotic Male Veterans at the Veterans Hospital, Northrup, New York," *The Journal of Nervous and Mental Disease* 113(1) (1951), 247; Maurice Klotz, Wallace Ritchie, Burtrum Schiele, "Prefrontal Lobotomy: A Clinical Survey of 100 Cases Given an Active Retraining Program in a Mental Hospital," *Psychiatric Quarterly* 26(1) (January 1952); Paul McReynolds and Marion Weide, "The Prediction and Assessment of Psychological Changes Following Prefrontal Lobotomy," *Journal of Mental Science* 105 (1959), 971–78; Donald W. Black, "Psychosurgery," *Southern Medical Journal* 75(4) (April 1982), 453–58; J. Ball, C.J. Klett and C.J. Gresock, "The Veterans Administration Study of Prefrontal Lobotomy," *Journal of Clinical and Experimental Psychopathology* 20 (1959), 205–17; Carol K. Redmond and Theodore Colton, eds., *Biostatistics in Clinical Trials* (New York: John Wiley and Sons, 2001), 99–100; Peter Sterling, "Ethics and Effectiveness of Psychosurgery" in *Controversy in Psychiatry*, John Paul Brady and H. Keith Brodie, eds. (Philadelphia, PA: W.B. Saunders Co., 1978); "Psychosurgery Effects Still Linger," *The Washington Post*, April 6, 1980, A1.

28. B. Blassingille, "Rehabilitation of Negro Post-Leukotomy Patients," *Journal of Nervous and Mental Disease* 121(6) (1955), 527.

and less than ten percent of the veterans were discharged from the hospital.[29] An unbiased observer would consider those adverse reactions to be an indication of the failure of the method. The shock treatments and lobotomies inflicted upon our veterans post World War II seem unreal, the stuff of movies. And one classic movie based in a mental hospital, *One Flew Over the Cuckoo's Nest,* actually had fictional characters who were veterans. Chief Bromden is a Native American World War II vet, supposedly with over 100 electric shock treatments; Randle McMurphy, the protagonist, who is eventually lobotomized, was a Korean War vet and POW. Sadly, the experiences of these fictional characters were not that divorced from the reality of that era.[30]

Psychological aftereffects of war were only part of the veteran's problem when he returned to civilian life. A home of one's own was a commonly held dream among the returning soldiers. In the early days after the war, however, it was a difficult dream to realize. New housing construction had lagged during the Depression, and industrial production during the 1940s had concentrated on the war effort. More than a million newly married couples, my parents among them, found themselves living with extended family. Even if there was housing available, a vet found it difficult to get a job. Unemployment was high, and, in comparison to civilian men, veterans were three times as likely to be without work. My father struggled to find work; his paratrooper skills of jumping from an airplane, operating a Browning automatic rifle and being a platoon scout were not transferable to the American workforce. After a brief foray into the private sector as a department store detective, Dad rejoined the Army in 1947, becoming a Counterintelligence Agent, achieving some measure of job stability.

Marital satisfaction was another victim of the war. GIs may have married in record numbers, but many of these unions were star-crossed. The divorce rate skyrocketed. While marriages may have dramatically increased in the immediate aftermath of war, so did divorce, belying the image of all those happy marriages of the Greatest Generation. The postwar divorce rate was at its highest ever in 1946, with 4.3 divorces for

---

29. Hanna Moser, "A Ten Year Follow-up of Lobotomy Patients," *Hospital and Community Psychiatry* 20 (December 1969), 381.

30. Ken Kesey, *One Flew Over the Cuckoo's Nest* (New York: Viking Press, 1962).

every one thousand marriages.[31] These dissolutions occurred in an era before the advent of no-fault divorce. So, as with my parents, one party had to assign blame to the other partner to obtain the divorce, which, as I know from personal experience, only made family life more contentious. Adultery, desertion, habitual drunkenness, and cruel and inhuman treatment were just a few of the accusations made in order to end a union. Divorce rates slowly declined from that high point after World War II, during and after the Korean War, and into the 1960s and early 1970s. The 1946 record was not equaled and surpassed until 1973, during the Vietnam War. Men of the Greatest Generation era who had seen combat during World War II were more likely to divorce than noncombat veterans or men who had not served. The alienation that I felt as a child, coming from a "broken home," would not have been as severe had I been aware that so many other families were not living the postwar American dream either.

Many have posited that the GI Bill solved all the postwar troubles. It has been heralded as changing everything for the returning veteran, making him feel like a first-class citizen and inspiring his lifelong involvement in civic organizations. The Servicemen's Readjustment Act of 1944 did provide some with the opportunity to obtain an education which would have been impossible to achieve. However, the majority of veterans had not taken advantage of the law within five years after the war.[32] Forty percent were utilizing it, but men with a young family, like my father, could not survive without a full-time job. My father did not get a college degree until 1968, after his divorce from my mother, as his children struggled their way through high school and college.

The facts belie the common assumptions of the fate of the Greatest Generation upon their return. Reality is mixed. While it was a victorious war, there were still hurdles to be overcome. Impressions of a supportive community ready to hear graphic war stories of combat are just that, impressions. According to my Dad, no one wanted to know the

31. Derek W. Little and William L. Anderson, "All's Fair: War and Other Causes of Divorce from a Beckerian Perspective: Statistical Data Included," *American Journal of Economics and Sociology* 58(4) (October 1999), 901–22; See also, E. Palko and Glen Elder, "World War II and Divorce: A Life-course Perspective," *American Journal of Sociology* 95(5) (1990), 1213–234.

32. Michael J. Bennett, *When Dreams Came True: The GI Bill and the Making of Modern America* (Washington, D.C., Brassey's, 1996), 205; See also, Suzanne Mettler, *Soldiers to Citizens: The GI Bill and the Making of the Greatest Generation* (New York: Oxford University Press, 2005).

truth about the horrors of war. Just like with subsequent generations of soldiers, the public wanted the glory and symbols, parades and yellow ribbons, leaving the darker side of war, embodied by invisible wounds, ignored for the most part, even today. It simplifies matters if society can have an unblemished image of a good war where everyone sacrificed and did their duty with honor. As Thomas Childers, son of a World War II veteran and nephew of an airman who died in the last American plane shot down over Nazi Germany, said in *Soldier from the War Returning: The Troubled Homecoming of the Greatest Generation,* "This reassuring, uncomplicated portrait has been repeated so often in public commemorations and memorial addresses that it has become almost an incantation, more liturgical than historical."[33]

33. Thomas Childers, *Soldier From the War Returning: The Greatest Generation's Troubled Homecoming From World War II* (New York: Houghton-Mifflin-Harcourt, 2009), 5.

8

EVEN HEROES CRY

A nation reveals itself not only by the men it produces but also by the men it honors, the men it remembers.

—President John F. Kennedy,
Amherst College, October 26, 1963

It wasn't anything they said because they said nothing; it was almost as if they were brooding over a huge secret that they kept to themselves only because it wouldn't help to tell anyone. They were part of a dreadful community that no one else could penetrate and that they couldn't escape.

—Carsten Jensen, *We the Drowned*

A haunting question arises every time a war hero falls. In April 2011, a chorus of whys arose when Clay Hunt, a handsome, vibrant veteran of Iraq and Afghanistan, died from a self-inflicted gunshot. This personable former Marine was a veterans' advocate. Hunt had appeared in a public service announcement on suicide prevention. He was doing everything right to fight his demons of war, seeking counseling and surrounding himself with family and friends, but ultimately, there was no escape, no refuge from the ghosts of four close comrades who had been killed in combat.[1] Research has shown that suicides of active duty and war veterans of Afghanistan and Iraq have consistently increased. A 2021 report stated that 30,177 veterans of those wars died by suicide. Those rates were "four times higher" than deaths from military operations in those two wars. (uso.org/stories/2664/military)

---

1. "One big question haunts Marine's suicide: Why?" CNN.com, accessed April 14, 2011, www.cnn.com/2011/US/04/14california.marine.suicide/index.html.

Paltry efforts at reintegrating our combat veterans have been a hall-mark of our nation's welcome home routine. Once the yellow ribbons are stained and frayed, and the parades and speeches are over, heroes fade from public view.

The aftermath of World War II was no different. Feel-good stories about our brave military men filled the newspapers during and after the war. Singled out for special praise were those valorous men who won the Medal of Honor (MOH), all four hundred and sixty-four of them. Two hundred and sixty-six MOHs were awarded posthumously so that the one hundred and ninety-eight who returned home were accorded singular admiration.[2] Successful lives followed for many, such as United States Senator Daniel Inouye, a Japanese American, who, despite a grenade hit that severely wounded him, led his platoon in Italy in a successful action to capture an artillery and mortar post. Some of these brave heroes struggled when they returned home, but that darker tale is little known. Audie Murphy, Commando Kelly, Junior Spurrier, Pappy Boyington and Ira Hayes were all household names during World War II, glorified for their war valor.

Audie Murphy was the most decorated soldier of World War II, with the Medal of Honor, Distinguished Service Cross, Silver Star, Legion of Merit, and two Bronze Stars among his awards for valor in Italy and France. Murphy, a soldier with the 15th Infantry, was credited with killing over two hundred and forty Nazis in the battle where he won his highest award. The MOH citation detailed his heroism:

> With the enemy tanks abreast of his position, 2d Lt. Murphy climbed on the burning tank destroyer, which was in danger of blowing up at any moment, and employed its .50 caliber machinegun against the enemy. He was alone and exposed to German fire from 3 sides, but his deadly fire killed dozens of Germans and caused their infantry attack to waver. The enemy tanks, losing infantry support, began to fall back. For an hour, the Germans tried every available weapon to eliminate 2d Lt. Murphy, but he continued to hold his position and wiped out

---

2. "Medal of Honor statistics," U.S. Army Center of Military History, accessed May 15, 2011, http://www.history.army.mil/html/moh/mohstats.html.

a squad which was trying to creep up unnoticed on his right flank. Germans reached as close as 10 yards, only to be mowed down by his fire. He received a leg wound but ignored it and continued the single-handed fight until his ammunition was exhausted. He then made his way to his company, refused medical attention, and organized the company in a counterattack that forced the Germans to withdraw.[3]

Murphy, with his boyish good looks and legacy of unimaginable courage, came home to a hero's welcome in June 1945. Military top brass and a huge victory parade awaited him in San Antonio, Texas. Soon, there was a feature piece in *Life* magazine on July 16, 1945, with a photograph of Audie on the cover. With his freckled face and radiant smile, the young soldier seemed carefree and content, but beneath that pleasant demeanor was a traumatized man who would never find peace. Plagued by insomnia, nightmares, and anxiety, his postwar years were far from carefree. A short-lived marriage immediately after the war was just one of the casualties of his erratic moods and depression. His first wife, Wanda Hendrix, obtained a divorce on mental cruelty grounds.[4] Next, Audie married Pamela Archer in 1951. Despite his womanizing, excessive gambling, and addiction to the sleeping pill Olacidyl, this union lasted until his untimely death in 1971.[5]

Revenue to support Murphy's outsized lifestyle came from his Hollywood movies, mainly Westerns, the most successful of which was a semi-autobiographical *To Hell and Back* 1955 movie based on his war exploits. On television, Murphy starred in a short-lived series, *Whispering Smith*, which only aired twenty episodes. By the late sixties, the World War II hero had been forgotten. His film career, which had been going downhill for years, stalled completely. In 1968, he was declared bankrupt. In 1970, Murphy was arrested on a charge of assault with intent to commit murder after an altercation about a dog training fee charged to one of his girlfriends. Audie had numerous girlfriends during his marriage to the

3. "Audie Murphy's Medal of Honor Citation," *The Price of Freedom: Americans at War*, accessed March 10, 2011, http://americanhistory.si.edu/militaryhistory/collection/object.asp?ID=421.
4. Charles Whiting, *Hero: The Life and Death of Audie Murphy* (Chelsea, MI: Scarborough House, 1990), 167–203.
5. Whiting, 241–43.

long-suffering Pam.[6] In an April 14, 2010, *Los Angeles Daily News* article after Pam Murphy's death, his widow was quoted as having said, "Even with the desertion and adultery at the end, he still remained my hero."[7] By the time Pam died, Audie had been gone nearly four decades. His turbulent life ended prematurely and tragically on May 23, 1971, when a small plane carrying Murphy on a business trip crashed into the side of a Virginia mountain near Roanoke. Audie and four other passengers died, along with the ineffective pilot, Herman Butler. Butler was not instrument qualified and had two prior aviation suspensions, once for crash landing a plane that had run out of gas. Murphy's plane was the target of a massive search. After the crash, a week passed before the wreckage was spotted and the bodies were recovered.[8]

The life of Audie Murphy ended at the age of forty-six. An incompetent pilot had succeeded where hundreds of Germans had failed. In reality, though, his life had been irrevocably shattered decades before on the battlegrounds of Italy and France. The media reporting his death focused on the war hero angle. Audie had suffered from his iconic hero status and spoke openly about his postwar struggles, but Audie, as the war victim, did not fit into the narrative America had constructed about World War II. In June 1971, *Time* magazine memorialized him in an essay, *Heroes: To Hell and Not Quite Back,* a rare realistic description of America's most decorated soldier of World War II.[9]

Audie Murphy may have been the most prominent of the World War II Medal of Honor winners to struggle with war trauma, but he was not the only one. Charles Kelly, the first enlisted man to win the Medal in Europe, died in 1985 of liver and kidney failure, his heroic legacy unknown to those treating him at the Veterans hospital in his hometown of Pittsburgh, Pennsylvania, a city that had honored and feted him four decades prior. Kelly, in the heady postwar days, had the moniker "Commando," descriptive of his MOH battle exploits in Italy. Kelly had single-handedly defended an ammunition depot from German attack, using a Browning automatic rifle, a Tommy gun, 66 mm mortar shells for grenades and a bazooka to stop the enemy. His actions gave American

---

6. Whiting, 250–54.
7. Dennis McCarthy, "Pam Murphy, widow of actor Audie Murphy was veterans' friend and advocate," *Los Angeles Daily News*, April 14, 2010.
8. Whiting, 255–58.
9. Whiting, 259.

troops cover to escape the depot. Fresh out of training, Kelly had just joined the 36th infantry four days earlier. His division landed at Paestum in the Gulf of Salerno and linked up with 82nd Airborne paratroopers. The landing and jump were the Allies' initial forays into fierce fighting with Germans in mainland Italy. Kelly continued to fight with the 36th up the boot of Italy in battles for San Pietro and Cassino.[10]

After the army brought Kelly back, early in the spring of 1944, the war hero was showered with tributes and accolades. Pittsburgh declared April 25, 1944, "Commando Kelly Day," celebrated his arrival with a motorcade, and presented him with a gold key to the city. Thousands turned out to welcome back their hometown boy. Shortly thereafter, Kelly was sent across the country on a "Here's Your Infantry" tour with other decorated infantrymen to sell war bonds. The humble soldier from Pittsburgh was treated like a star. The Saturday Evening Post gave him $15,000 for his story, and Twentieth Century Fox added another $25,000 to his coffers for movie rights. Much of his new found money was squandered during the war bonds tour. Booked in high-priced hotels by the Army because of his high profile, Kelly paid most of the costs himself, the Army per diem of six dollars a day barely covering his chewing tobacco.

Meanwhile, Kelly had married Mae Boisch in 1945, shortly before his discharge from the service. A daughter was soon born, and being a new family man, Kelly decided to lease and operate a Sun Oil gas station. The business thrived at first because of his fame, but it wasn't long before misfortune struck. The station was robbed. Kelly went further into debt, partially because of ill-advised loans to family members, and more catastrophes were yet to come. Shortly after the Kelly son was born, his young wife, Mae, developed uterine cancer. Kelly spent thousands of dollars for her treatment, but to no avail. Mae died in 1951 at the age of twenty-five. Commando's money had run out. His home went into foreclosure. With no home, no job, and no wife, Kelly could no longer care for his two children. His daughter and son were sent to live with relatives. Mae's death was not the only family loss for Kelly in the early fifties. His youngest brother Danny had wanted to follow in Commando's footsteps and be a war hero. Since Danny was only seventeen, he needed an age waiver to enlist. Charles Kelly signed, and Danny was sent to Korea as an

10. "Charles Kelly," Military Times, Hall of Valor, accessed February 19, 2011, http://militarytimes.com/citations-medals=wards/recipient.php?recipientid=390.

infantry replacement. One week after he arrived in the war zone, Danny was reported as missing in action. His body was never recovered. Kelly felt intense guilt about his brother.

At one point, Kelly attempted to get his life back on track. Name recognition and his war hero status helped him get a political job in 1952. While traveling cross country campaigning for Dwight Eisenhower for President, Kelly reconnected with a girl, Betty Gaskins, whom he had met at Fort Knox in 1945. Soon, Charles and Betty married combined the children from their previous marriages, and had three more together. After his remarriage, Kelly continued to struggle. Alcoholism, his inability to keep a job, and his tendencies towards a rootless lifestyle accelerated, and his second marriage ended in divorce. He had little contact with his children. Classic symptoms of PTSD dogged Kelly throughout his life, but as was common for the World War II combat veteran, understanding the toll of war was practically nonexistent.[11]

Mike Wallace interviewed "Commando" on June 30th, 1957, and introduced Kelly as follows:

> Congressional Medal of Honor winner Commando Kelly was called a 'one-man army' during the Second World War. A tough kid from the wrong side of the tracks, shy Charles "Commando" Kelly, in just one of his battles, manned machine guns, rifles and an anti-tank gun in virtual single-handed defense of an ammunition dump and emerged unscratched. But in peacetime, Commando's been hit hard by bad-luck, ill-health, and financial misfortune. Let's try to find out why Chuck Kelly has failed to reap the rewards of heroism.[12]

Junior Spurrier is yet another soldier who "failed to reap the rewards of heroism." He was called the "Sergeant York of World War II" by *Stars and Stripes* after he won both the Distinguished Service Cross and the Medal of Honor for battlefield exploits in France. Spurrier mounted a tank and peppered the enemy with a machine gun. The young staff sergeant, a

11. Steve Levin, "North Side's battlefield hero found life's wounds too deep," *Pittsburgh Post Gazette*, May 31, 1999.

12. The Mike Wallace Interview—Guest: Charles "Commando" Kelly, June 30, 1957, accessed April 10, 2011, www.hrc.utexas.edu/multimedia/video/2008/Wallace/Kelly_commando_t.html.

platoon commander in the 134th Infantry, 35th division, then led his men in the capture of a hill near Lay St. Christopher, France, in September 1944. Spurrier was responsible for taking twenty-two Nazis prisoner in that action, which resulted in his Distinguished Service Cross, the second highest military honor bestowed by the Army for combat. A few short months later, near Achain, France, Spurrier advanced alone into town from the west while the rest of G Company entered from the east. During the attack with a variety of weapons that included a Browning Automatic Rifle (BAR), rocket launchers, and hand grenades, Spurrier killed twenty-five Germans and took four more prisoners. Given the Medal of Honor for almost single-handedly capturing that small village in France's Moselle Valley, Spurrier was lauded for valor and for bringing honor to the United States Armed Forces.[13]

Six years later, amid another war, the Army was no longer lauding Spurrier for honor and duty. When Junior returned home to West Virginia in 1945, he was greeted by a large "Heroes Day Parade." Twenty thousand enthusiastic supporters turned out to greet their hometown boy. A gala followed the parade, the Heroes Day dinner dance, where Junior met his wife. However, after the rousing welcome home, Spurrier was just another former soldier who had trouble adjusting, and he went back to where he was most successful: the Army. After reenlisting, he never regained his former glory. His drinking and alcohol abuse caused problems and setbacks. By the time the Korean War broke out Spurrier had been busted to the lowly rank of private. He refused to go to Korea and back into combat. Spurrier then went AWOL, which created a dilemma for the Army. Should they court-martial one of their most highly decorated World War II soldiers? The consensus was to give Spurrier a general discharge instead of military punishment to avoid embarrassment and media attention. This general designation, instead of an honorable discharge separation, is chosen when the negative aspects of the individual's service outweigh the positives in the soldier's performance of duty.

The next two decades of Junior's life continued to be turbulent. Repeated imprisonments for a variety of crimes, including attempted murder, concealed weapons charges, and obtaining money under false pretenses, show that Spurrier had not been able to leave violence behind after the war.

13. Bill Archer, "Paying tribute to a one-man Army," *Bluefield Daily Telegraph*, June 25, 2006.

In 1971, Spurrier's last stint in jail ended when the West Virginia governor, Arch A. Moore, Jr., ordered him released by executive decision. In 1977, Spurrier left the state for good and moved to a cabin in an isolated part of Tennessee to be near his daughter. He died in 1984 at the age of sixty-one. Because of Spurrier's postwar struggles, his legacy was overlooked in his home state for decades. Finally, in 2006, the For Those Who Served Museum in Mercer County, West Virginia, gave Spurrier the honor that was his due. A ceremony to unveil the Spurrier Memorial was held. His former wife attended and donated his Purple Heart and Bronze Star.[14]

Gregory "Pappy" Boyington was another Medal of Honor winner who was honored by top military brass and Presidents for his wartime exploits. His long-term postwar legacy was more complicated. Born in Couer d'Alene, Idaho, Pappy had had a rough life even prior to the war. His parents divorced soon after his birth, and his mother's second husband was an alcoholic.[15] Pappy thought that his abusive stepfather was his biological father until he enlisted in the Marines in the 1930s and found his birth certificate. Although Pappy had never had a relationship with his birth father, at this point, he took his name. Once in the Marines, Pappy trained to be a Naval aviator. This move stood him in good stead for his next career choice, the Flying Tigers.[16] This organization was a civilian air group contracted by Madame Chiang Kai-shek, the First Lady of the Republic of China. Also known as the American Volunteer Group (AVG), that coterie of fliers, which Pappy joined in 1941, was engaged in protecting China against Japanese aggression in World War II. Being involved in air battles over Burma, China, Thailand, and French Indo-China provided Pappy with valuable combat experience, something America was lacking when it entered World War II.

When the AVG disbanded in 1942, Pappy was reinstated into the Marine Corps. With his civilian combat experience, Pappy was the perfect man to be the Commanding Officer of Marine Fighter Squadron 214, popularly known as the "Black Sheep Squadron." Pappy, a fearless aviator, engaged in many firefights with the Japanese in the Pacific, including the Russell Islands and Bougainville. Pappy tied the American

---

14. James H. Willbanks, ed., *America's Heroes: Medal of Honor Winners from the Civil War to Afghanistan* (Santa Barbara, CA: ABC-CLIO, 2011), 321.

15. Bruce Gamble, *Black Sheep One: The Life of Gregory 'Pappy' Boyington* (Novato, CA: Presidio, 2000), 5–10.

16. Gamble, 119–23, 137.

record of enemy planes downed on January 3, 1944, a memorable and also unfortunate day for Pappy. On his record-breaking day, Pappy himself was shot down by the enemy near the island of Rabaul.[17] Seriously injured and floundering in the water, he was picked up by a Japanese submarine. Thus began twenty months of suffering for Pappy.

Much of his time was spent at Ofuna, a prison camp known for the brutality and torment of airmen and submariners brought to the "torture farm." Ofuna was a high-level interrogation prison run by the Japanese Navy. Hidden from the Red Cross, the men enslaved there were not registered as prisoners of war, so their fate remained unknown to their families.[18] Pappy was not released from Ofuna until after the Japanese surrender. He returned home to a hero's welcome and was personally awarded his Medal of Honor at the White House by President Harry Truman. Prior to the Presidential ceremony, Pappy had already been given the Navy Cross by the Commandant of the Marine Corps. After his awards were bestowed, Pappy traveled the country on a Victory Bond tour, a public relations tool to raise money to pay off war debt. During this tour, Pappy's postwar problems became obvious. He drank heavily and embarrassed the military. He was medically retired in 1947 at the age of thirty-three, despite having passed a comprehensive flight physical just seven months prior.[19] Stories of failed marriages, financial instability, and heavy drinking dominated the postwar news of Pappy. An offer of a television series in the mid-nineteen seventies, based on Pappy's 1958 autobiography *Baa Baa Black Sheep,* was a welcome turn of fortune.

Black Sheep Squadron starred Robert Conrad as Pappy and portrayed Marine aviators as a rough, brawling group who took incredible risks. The two-year television run of the series placed Pappy in the public eye once again, this time in a more positive light. During the final decade of Pappy's life, he became more settled, made occasional TV appearances, and appeared at air shows.[20] While married to his fourth and final wife, a recovering alcoholic herself, his drinking had somewhat abated. Long periods of sobriety ensued, but he was never able to conquer his alcoholism completely. Pappy's relationships with his three children, the products of

17. Gamble, 238, 289–307.
18. Gamble, 320–28.
19. Gamble, 352, 356, 366–67.
20. Gamble, 394–406.

his first marriage, were fractured. His sole paternal relationship was with his eldest, his only son, who became a colonel in the Air Force. Pappy's two daughters were not part of his life. His youngest daughter had been adopted by her maternal aunt and uncle and had no communication with her father. His other daughter died in 1971 at the age of thirty-four of an apparent suicide.[21] Pappy was a lifelong heavy smoker, and in 1988, Pappy died of lung cancer and was given a military funeral at Arlington.

However, the controversy over Pappy did not end with his death. A debate about his legacy continued into the early twenty-first century. Veterans in Coeur d'Alene, Idaho, Pappy's birthplace, lobbied the Kootenai County Commission to change the name of the city airport to "Pappy Boyington Airfield" in honor of the Medal of Honor hero, but the vets encountered resistance. The county commissioners refused to vote on the proposal. Much of the furor and disapproval centered on Pappy's lifestyle after the war. It took more than a year, and the election of new commissioners before the measure came to a vote and was finally approved.[22] Even many decades after the war, there was still a lack of recognition that Pappy's turbulent postwar life was probably related to PTSD and not a personal failing.

Ira Hayes was not a World War II Medal of Honor winner, but his name might be as recognizable to the modern American public as Audie Murphy's. As one of the men in the iconic Joe Rosenthal photograph of the Iwo Jima flag raising, Ira's tale has been told in song and on the big screen. Johnny Cash's mournful cover of the folk singer Peter La Farge's song, "The Ballad of Ira Hayes," captures Ira's anguish in song. *The Outsider,* a 1960s television show, and the *Flags of Our Fathers* film (based on the book of the same name) in 2006 filled in the outlines of the Native American Marine's life, which began on the Gila River Indian Reservation near Scottsdale, Arizona. The Gila River had already begun to run dry by the time of Ira's birth in 1923. Ira's tribe, the Pima Indians, had been settled in Southern Arizona for centuries, successfully farming fertile soil irrigated with water from the once-teeming river. However, the government destroyed the Pima way of life with ill-advised dams and building projects. As the river dried up, poverty resulted. Ira's grade

---

21. Gamble, 381, 386, 411.

22. "Pappy Boyington Field: A campaign to honor a hero," accessed May 6, 2011, www.pappyboyingtonfield.com.

school years were spent in a reservation school for Indian children. When it was time for high school, he was sent to a boarding school, as was the custom with Indian teenagers, in order to Americanize them.[23]

The year after Pearl Harbor, Ira completed his high school education and enlisted in the Marines, in spite of objections by his family. A tough, crack sharpshooter, his next step was the para-marines. Ira excelled in spite of the grueling training regimen. Wings proudly affixed to his uniform, Ira took great pleasure in being a Marine paratrooper. Bougainville was a ferocious, hot and deadly place. Ira first tasted combat there, killing a man close up. Ira was sitting in a foxhole, guarding his buddy, and bayoneted an enemy soldier who was ready to kill his sleeping friend. Voices of the dead probably already haunted Ira when he landed next on Iwo Jima, the island that would memorialize Ira's place in history. Ira was part of the first wave that arrived on that beach, into hell. Iwo Jima was strewn with body parts. Men had been sliced in half by a hail of bullets. Wounded and dying Marines screamed and cried for their mothers. At the end of the battle on the first day, more than 3,500 Americans had been either killed or wounded. It was three more horrifying days before the strategic Mount Surabachi fell. Control of the volcanic peak was key in order to deprive the Japanese of a lookout and artillery post.

After the conquest of Surabachi, Marine Colonel Chandler Johnson ordered an American flag hoisted high. He directed Staff Sergeant Louis Lowrey to photograph that moment for inclusion in *Leatherneck* magazine, a Marine monthly. Secretary of the Navy James Forrestal had just arrived on the beach during the initial raising. Forrestal demanded that the flag be brought to him as a souvenir. However, Colonel Johnson was a fiery and loyal commander who wanted that flag for his Marines, who had shed so much blood on the barren island. Another flag was quickly rustled up, and a different group of six Marines was sent up to the mountaintop for a second photo of the colors. That flag was given to Forrestal. Associated Press photographer Joe Rosenthal preserved that second raising. It became an iconic picture that assured that Ira Hayes, along with the other five Marines, would be symbols of World War II heroism after their photo had been splashed all over American newspapers. The public reacted with pride because the Marines had succeeded in conquering Iwo

---

23. James Bradley with Ron Powers, *Flags of Our Fathers* (New York: Bantam Books, 2000), 38, 76–78.

Jima. The patriotic glow, however, was a bit premature. The battle had not ended with Mount Surabachi. Four more weeks of bitter fighting ensued, with thousands more casualties, until Iwo Jima was secure, a fact that received little press attention.[24]

Three of the flag raisers in the Rosenthal picture were dead, killed during that bloody month after the photo's publication. Ira and the other remaining survivors, John Bradley and Rene Gagnon were ordered back to America in May 1945 for a war bond tour. The two Marines and the Navy Corpsman were the prime attractions in a government public relations campaign for money to finance the war effort. Ira only lasted a few weeks on the tour. He drank heavily every night to deal with his war demons, and he was quickly becoming an embarrassment to the top military. The Marines soon sent him back overseas until the war ended. Ira further descended into alcoholism after his return home. Postwar news of Ira had nothing to do with heroism; rather, he often made the papers in Arizona for his drunk and disorderly arrests. After Ira's move to Chicago, he took a job as a tool grinder at International Harvester. Aware of his troubles, in 1953, a Chicago newspaper sponsored a "Save Ira Hayes" fund to help raise money to send him to an alcoholism treatment sanitarium. The *Chicago Sun-Times* headline deemed him cured after his short stay of a few days, but Ira Hayes was never "cured." His "war" did not end until a frigid day in January 1955 when he was found lying dead in a ditch on the reservation. The official cause of death was alcohol poisoning and exposure.[25]

Murphy, Kelly, Spurrier, Boyington, and Hayes were all recognized during World War II as heroes. All five were subjected to scorn and criticism after the war ended because they failed to remain on the pedestal on which America had placed them. Many, many decades later, there finally may be the recognition that their disappointing, sometimes tragic, postwar lives were not because of a defect of character, or failure of nerve. The battles that brought these heroes accolades and glory also left them with trauma and despair. For some combat veterans, all the parades, ticker tape and marching bands could not drown out the cries of their lost brothers in arms.

24. Bradley, 197–205.
25. Bradley, 324–33.

9

THOSE DAMN BOOTS

It all began with the boots, dark brown, slightly scuffed, with the name "Schultz" inked inside. Hidden in an out-of-the-way corner of my uncle's clothes closet for forty years. None of my aging relatives could remember how they got there. The paratrooper boots were my father's, found by my maternal aunt when she was performing the sad task of sorting through her husband's belongings after his death in October 1998. She handed them to me after I arrived at her home, saying, "They're your father's. You should keep them."

That evening, I excitedly called Dad in California and told him of the unlikely find. My father could never recall what had become of his boots. It was a good possibility that during his 1958 divorce from my mother and his subsequent emotional difficulties, he had given away some of his war memorabilia.[1] I asked Dad if I could keep the boots for sentimental reasons, thinking that it would not be a problem; after all, he had given me his paratrooper ring, his wings, and his Longest Day rosary many years earlier and had donated to the World War II Museum in New Orleans the trench knife used to cut himself out of his parachute on D-Day. Dad agreed to let me keep the boots, albeit a bit reluctantly.

My father and I had rebuilt our close relationship over the past couple of decades, especially after my sister died in the 1970s. Dad's health had steadily gotten worse since the mid-1980s. At the age of sixty-two, he retired from his position as Clinical Director of the Army Drug and Alcohol Prevention Program at Fort Irwin in the California desert. After a diagnosis of emphysema and congestive heart failure, my father was tethered to an oxygen tank. Flying to the East Coast was difficult for him after 1985, so from the time my daughter was a toddler, she and I headed west every summer to spend a few weeks with Dad.

1. A German Lugar belonging to my father was found by my cousin, Margaret Russo, after the 2004 deaths of her parents. My uncle, the elder brother of my mother, who was also my godfather, had hidden it beneath boards in his garage, still loaded.

When I called my father a few days after the boot conversation, the iciness in his voice troubled me. I asked if there was a problem. He responded by telling me he was upset about his boots, but he did not want to discuss it. He had written me a letter, and I was to reply to him in writing. Stunned, I challenged him, the former therapist, about his unusual and out-of-character behavior. My voice trembling, I demanded that he read me the letter over the phone. He quickly agreed, even though his wife was telling him to let me wait until it came in the mail. I had no idea what dynamics were going on between the two of them, especially when Dad came back and whispered out of earshot of his wife, "I'm really proud of you, baby, for standing up for yourself." Then he socked me in the gut with his letter:

> I really don't want to write this letter because I'm not sure that
> you will understand either my intent or the quality of my love
> for you . . . I have no illusions about being a Norman Rockwell
> type of father and grandfather to both you and Rosemary . . .
> What really hurts me is the way, you set me up regarding my
> paratrooper boots. When you told me about them, I said I
> would like to have them, and I would replace them with boots
> I recently purchased. Your response was that you wanted them
> because the only things that I have ever given you were my
> rosary and my ring, and because of this obvious shortcoming,
> you wanted these boots. Because of the punctuated way you
> made the statement, I agreed that you could have them, and
> then I started wondering why I felt so lousy. I came to realize
> that, directly or indirectly, you were "laying a guilt trip on me."
> As a matter of fact, you were angry with me. I can only assume
> that the pain I cause (sic) you and your sister because of my
> alcoholism and all of its consequences is a part of this situation.
> God only knows how I have tried to make that up . . . I don't
> know if you remember that when I was in the beginning stages
> of my recovery from alcoholism . . . I wrote you and your sister
> a letter telling you . . . that we could not keep on corresponding
> if you, but particularly your mother and sister were going to
> keep berating me about what a no-good "son of a bitch" I was.

At that time, I don't think that you, your mother and your sister ever knew or even cared that I was a drink away from a drunk. I had little, if any, "self-respect" left. Remember the Christmas I met you coming down the stairs in handcuffs? I don't ever remember you taking a stand on this injustice, but I accepted it because you were your mother's daughter. I am not trying to hurt, but I do want you to know that I have accepted some of what I consider your shortcomings because of my love for you. I request that you send me my paratrooper boots so that I might enjoy looking at them, feel them, shine them, and maybe even wear them a few more times. I consider the rosary and the ring to be much more historical and significant than a pair of boots. I remind you, too, that I have given you more than these two items . . . you have my paratrooper wings . . . I want you to know that I have always loved you and will continue to love you regardless of how you react to this letter . . . Since we can't resolve this issue face to face, I prefer doing it via the mails.[2]

Blindsided, I tried to catch my breath. All the confusion, hurt, and fear from my teenage years came flooding back. I couldn't understand the reason for my father's tirade. In an attempt to defend my request, I explained that I had only wanted the boots for sentimental reasons and told him that as no object was worth fighting over, I would put the boots in the mail to him the next day. Tremendously hurt by my father's unexpected accusations, I tried to regain my emotional equilibrium. During the confrontational post-divorce early years, I had tried to stay out of the fray. While living with my mother and her extended family nearby, I would hear criticisms of my father, most often from my immigrant grandmother, who had no sympathy for his war trauma. I would defend him, but usually, I had no allies. The three-year gap during my late teens, when I barely heard from my father, had made me feel sad, abandoned, and insecure. However, when Dad returned to Philadelphia in 1967, I asked him to walk me down the aisle at my wedding that year. Even then, parental conflict impacted my big day. My father and mother sat ten

---

2. Arthur Schultz to Carol Schultz Vento, personal letter, November 1, 1998, personal files of Carol Schultz Vento.

feet away from each other in the church pew during the ceremony. Dad refused to attend my reception that evening since his second wife was not welcome, according to my mother's directive, and neither of my parents would compromise on that issue.

After Dad received the boots, I called him to ask why he was so angry with me. He said, "You didn't do enough when your mother was divorcing me to stop it," the statement of a desperate man who never really accepted the loss of his family despite his two additional marriages. I responded, "But, Dad, I was only eleven years old and wasn't quite sure what was happening." I reminded him that it had taken two years after the initial break-up for my parent's divorce to become final, during which there had been brief attempts at reconciliation. Dad's accusations in his letter that I did not care about or support him could not have been further from the truth. The handcuff incident he castigated me about in his letter had involved unpaid child support for my sister. On Christmas Eve 1968, I brought him a present. Two policemen were in his apartment flanking him when I arrived, waiting to take him to jail. "Your mother did this!" he snarled at me as they led him down the steps. I immediately left, frantically called my mother and Dad was released pronto. Being pulled back into a confrontation in middle age was emotionally draining. As an adult, defending my actions as a youngster whose parents were divorcing felt unfair and unwarranted. It placed me in a parental role, a reversal of the normal pattern. After a few more conversations, Dad apologized and told me that he hadn't been himself lately, but he didn't elaborate further as to the cause when I questioned him.

After the boot altercation, our relationship resumed its usual pattern, but a few years later, there was another conflagration. It happened in 2001 in a seedy room at the Tropicana Hotel in Los Vegas. While I was planning a Las Vegas trip, I offered to drive, with my daughter and cousin, one-hundred-plus miles across the desert to visit Dad and his wife at their California home. We had already picked a lodge nearby at which to stay. I was worried that Dad was not strong enough to travel. The deterioration of his health was accelerating. He could not walk very far, increasingly dependent upon stronger doses of oxygen to breathe, gasping for air if he was without it for even a few minutes. Even in his frail condition, they decided to drive over and meet us in Vegas.

We arrived a day before them. Our check-in at the Tropicana was a forerunner of the disaster the week would become. Our room reeked of smoke, the sheets were dirty, and the toilet broke our first night there. No other rooms were available, so we spent that night sleeping on top of the spreads. Later the next day, Dad and his wife arrived, and even though he was in a wheelchair, hooked to his canister, he seemed upbeat and happy to see us. The five of us socialized that evening at dinner and made plans to meet up for lunch the next day. My daughter had a hair appointment across town that morning, and we got delayed at the salon, so I called and said we would meet them in a while. By the time we met up with W and Dad that afternoon, her demeanor was frosty. When we arrived in their cramped, dank room, later preparing to leave for dinner, she lashed out at me. "You don't want to be with us." My cousin just sat there, mouth agape. My daughter started crying. The bizarre scene ended with Dad attempting to calm me down. I was hyperventilating, trying to explain myself, but to no avail. The three of us finally left, with my Dad distressed. The next day, I called their room, only to find out that they had checked out that morning, three days early, without even letting me know.

A few days later, I returned East and called their house. W, a stewardess, was away on a flight. Dad asked me to apologize to W. At first, I resisted since I felt I had done nothing wrong, but after some cajoling from him, I acquiesced. When W returned home, I told her that I hadn't meant to upset her; it wasn't intentional, and I was sorry. With that, I thought the Las Vegas incident was resolved. Over the next few months, W and I communicated politely when I called Dad, and then, nine months later, I received a letter from my father demanding another apology, stating that he and W were having a difficult time dealing with the Las Vegas affair.

I did not realize how much this matter hurt her. I carelessly compounded the issue by continuing to give her feelings that I was not supporting her by still maintaining my relationship with you by our numerous phone conversations which I now know have caused her doubts about my loyalty to her. As a matter of fact, we have talked about separation– this is not right!

Furthermore, you should realize that she is my wife. Aside from the fact that I love her— she has been my shelter in facing my remaining years . . . She has helped me stay afloat during a serious illness which ended up in a hospital. She is my lifesaver . . . has given me much more devotion & support than I have given her. Accordingly, I must tell you, as much as it saddens me, that I do not want any more communication with you until you resolve your differences. I know that you are working hard on refining your own emotional stability, but I hope you can see your way to help mend your relationship . . . Dad, with Love. P.S. I hope you can understand that I'm writing this with a heavy heart, but there should be no question that she is, first and foremost, the most important person in my life.[3]

After this latest scolding, I was ready to throw in the towel on the relationship with my father. Tired of reacting to turmoil, I withdrew and tried to sort out my emotions. Feelings of anger, resentment, abandonment, and bewilderment swirled about, pulling me back to the days of my teenage years. I had tried so hard to leave that behind. How dare he keep dictating the terms of our relationship! I was tired of being the one left out of the equation. As his only surviving child, I thought that the bond I had worked so hard at maintaining was unbreakable, but I was wrong. Dad seemed ready to throw me overboard to save himself. After a week or so, I decided to respond to him in writing, not wanting to get into recriminations on the phone. A response to my letter came from his wife, saying that my contrition was not sufficient—I must apologize once more. There I was, stuck in the middle once again. I just wanted to escape from dramatics, having spent my entire life trying to leave family patterns of the past behind. In my mind, I was the rational one, the family member who believed in dialogue and discussion to try to resolve differences, the intellectual who eschewed the emotional, overwrought way of family relating. Three months went by before I finally called my father. My resentment towards him gradually turned to worry. Finally, I grew tired of checking California obituaries daily to see if my father was

---

3. Arthur Schultz to Carol Schultz Vento, personal letter, July 13, 2002, personal files of Carol Schultz Vento.

still alive. I sympathized with his pain like I always had. Once again, I tried to understand the broken parts of my father. Swallowing my pride, I called and again apologized to his wife, even though I felt that I was being held hostage by the recent dynamics of anger that had arisen in my father's third marriage. Also, I was bewildered by his wife's actions. Our relationship had been pleasant for years. It seemed that as Dad's health deteriorated, the interactions between the two of them had gotten tense, and I had somehow gotten caught in the crossfire. I decided the best thing to do was surrender and accept the situation for the sake of my father. It was more important to me to stay connected to and supportive of him than it was for me to continue being righteous.

Three years after this 2002 drama, during my father's last year of life, he asked me to help him return to Philadelphia. He wanted to be closer to me and his granddaughter. But my Dad's health issues were accelerating. Breathing was even more difficult for him. His weight plummeted from his normal 160 to 120, and his lack of appetite was due to the severity of his chronic obstructive pulmonary disease (COPD). His wife resisted letting him go, and I knew that I would be in for a long battle to get Dad back to the Philadelphia area. He was ambivalent about putting me in the middle, saying he didn't want to be a burden, and I was torn about being in the middle of my father's marital relationship again, not wanting to have his final days fraught with conflict.

Moreover, I just was not able to deal with the emotional toll of another confrontation. As it turned out, Dad's health declined too rapidly for him to make any changes. He wouldn't return East until his urn was delivered to me on Halloween night, 2005. With my father finally at rest, I tried to make sense of what had caused the contention in his life during his last few years.

After my father's death, I began researching PTSD in the elderly World War II veteran in hopes of giving myself some peace of mind about his behavior. I knew that he loved me dearly. I was also aware that his poor health had put strains on his marriage, which had caused him additional emotional stress. Reading articles and studies on aging World War II veterans gave me some insight into my father's behavior. I began to understand that my elderly father's struggles were not unique. World War II was not only inextricably combined with my father's path

through life but also impacted the adjustment of millions of other soldiers. World War II overlaid the life choices and trajectories of so many
born in the first quarter of the twentieth century, benefiting some and
harming others.

In the retrospective report "When Nations Call," Richard Settersten
studied the pivotal role of military participation in World War II with its
attendant impact on family life. He evaluated the long-term physical and
mental health of those who served. Some men's lives had been changed for
the better. Settersten called the war a "structural intervention," a societal
upheaval that enabled many from poor and working-class backgrounds,
like my stepfather, to become middle class. The GI Bill provided an opportunity to obtain a college degree for those who would have never left
the farm, the village or the slum.[4] The positive aftereffects of World War
II have been emblazoned into the American consciousness. It is easier to
ignore the sadder aspects of the war legacy. The Greatest Generation narrative is diluted if there is an acknowledgment of the trauma that some
veterans dealt with following the war.

For World War II combat veterans especially, the negative aspects of
their war participation influenced both their physical and mental health.
Combat exposure not only increased the risk for PTSD. It is also related
to physical disability and chronic disease.[5] Cardiovascular risk, in particular, was associated with combat exposure, according to a report that
included World War II, Korean, and Vietnam War veterans. "Combat
veterans were four times more likely to be heavy drinkers, as opposed to
never drinkers than non-veterans, and 1.6 times more likely to be heavy
drinkers as opposed to never drinkers than non-combat veterans." Heavy
smoking was also strongly associated with combat, battle-scarred veterans having much higher rates in comparison with non-combat veterans
or civilians. The researchers noted that both drinking and smoking are
strongly associated with heart disease.[6]

4. Richard Settersten, Jr., "When Nations Call: How Wartime Military Service Matters for the Life
Course and Aging," *Research on Aging* 28(1) (January 2006), 13, 19.

5. Glen Elder, Jr., Elizabeth C. Clipp, James Scott Brown, Leslie Martin, and Howard W. Friedman,
"The LifeLong Mortality Risk of World War II Experiences," *Research on Aging* 31(4) (July 2009), 391–412.

6. "Male Combat Veterans Rank High in Heart Disease Risk," *Science Daily*, May 4, 2005, accessed
September 5, 2009, http://sciencedaily.com/releases/2005/05/050504003733.html; See also, Carla Johnson,
"Stress disorder may increase risk of heart problems," *Philadelphia Inquirer*, January 2, 2007.

Stress can also contribute to heart issues. Researchers from Harvard and Boston Universities analyzed data on World War II and Korean War veterans based on their responses to a questionnaire designed to measure PTSD symptoms. The veterans who reported more symptoms consistent with PTSD were more likely to have had a heart attack. Anxiety and tension can also contribute to dementia, an altered mental state with impaired functioning related to a disease of the brain. It has been demonstrated that elderly veterans of World War II and Korea have presented with symptoms of PTSD with the onset of dementia. Those signs of PTSD may have appeared for the first time in old age, or they may have reappeared after many years of quiescence in the veterans of those long-ago wars. Dementia lessens a veteran's ability to manage the traumatic memories of war. Those involved in combat were especially susceptible; the veterans with the most combat exposure were thirteen times more likely to have dementia-related PTSD as compared to non-combat veterans.[7] Studies on the physical health of World War II combat veterans are limited in number but highly suggestive of a link between the war and a more rapid physical decline.

The issue of psychological damage after World War II was covered in reports of "war neurosis" after the end of the war. However, most of these early studies tended to blame the victim. A great deal of attention was paid to the pre-military home background and environment of the soldier. Researchers in the 1940s and 1950s noted that heavy combat exposure could lead to postwar mental problems and neurotic symptoms but implied that those soldiers who broke down already had psychological weaknesses because of their history of having a difficult childhood.[8] Early analyses were directly influenced by the prevailing psychoanalytic theory, which concluded that those who had psychological problems from combat were already somewhat maladjusted, an assertion that was made but not necessarily proven by data. Very few studies were completed on the mental health of World War II veterans after the nineteen fifties,

7. "Traumatic Stress Disorder, Dementia Linked in WWII Vets," *Science Daily*, January 14, 2000, accessed September 5, 2009, http://www.sciencedaily.com/releases/200001/000113233143.htm

8. N.Q. Brill and G.W. Beebe, "A Follow-Up Study of War Neurosis," *VA Medical Monograph* (Washington, D.C.: Government Printing Office, 1955): See also, R.R. Grinker, B. Willerman, A.D. Bradley and A. Fastovsky, "A study of psychological predisposition to the development of operational fatigue: I. In officer flying personnel, II. In enlisted flying personnel," *American Journal of Orthopsychiatry* 16 (1946), 191, 214.

especially after the return of the warriors from Vietnam in the sixties and seventies, and attention shifted to their attendant psychological problems. A 1974 report on higher death rates of World War II soldiers who had been medically discharged for psychoneurosis in 1944 still focused on pathological personality types and maladjustment to explain the "excess mortality" of these men in the twenty years after WWII. Using data from men who had National Service Life Insurance (98% of World War II veterans) and finding mortality rates and causes from a VA Master Index, the researchers determined that situational combat factors were not dispositive of earlier death since the discharge papers of about half of the men who had been medically discharged stated that the neurosis existed prior to induction. The causes of early death for many of these men were alcoholism, suicide, cardiovascular disease, and tuberculosis.

Additionally, higher rates of homicide were also found. It is difficult to determine whether or not the statement on the 1944 discharge papers in regard to pre-existing neurosis was accurate. Looking at the causes of death retrospectively in 2011, an argument could be made that undiagnosed and untreated PTSD was related to "excess mortality."[9] It was not until the 1990s that the view regarding psychological suffering became more sympathetic towards veterans of the "good war."

Journalists, historians, and psychologists have belatedly shone a light on the emotional toll the trauma of war took on World War II veterans. *Newsweek* broached the subject in 1994 in an article related to the fiftieth anniversary of the D-Day invasion. The author pointed out that with all the ceremony and attention given to the D-Day veterans, "scarcely anyone has noted the continued, debilitating presence of PTSD among surviving veterans of World War II." The threat of death and helplessness experienced by them during the war was related to the persistence of memories or the appearance of intrusive, unwelcome images years after the war. Survivor's guilt and the inability to save a buddy loomed large. The reporter poignantly observed that "still under siege, the war's dream haunted veterans never do reach the foxhole" to save themselves or their buddies.[10]

_____

9. Robert J. Keehn, Irving D. Goldberg, and Gilbert W. Beebe, "Twenty-four Year Follow-up of Army Veterans with Disability Separation for Psychoneurosis in 1944," *Psychosomatic Medicine* 36(1) (January–February 1974).

10. David Gelman, "Reliving the painful past: The psychic suffering of many WWII soldiers went unrecognized for years," *Newsweek*, June 13, 1994, 20.

Mental health professionals were even slower than the media in recognizing the existence of late-life war-related PTSD in elderly veterans. In the 1990s, anecdotal evidence of this phenomenon finally began to be reported by clinicians, although hard data and empirical studies were still scarce. The few practitioners in the field who recognized the problem were not in agreement on the reasons for its late occurrence. Some posited that the celebratory homecoming environment was responsible—parades and warm welcomes supposedly put the trauma symptoms to rest, at least initially. Others thought that the explanation was the cultural pressure on the veterans to put the war behind them immediately when they returned home.[11]

Since a minority of the men who served in World War II were exposed to combat, it was easy for the societal denial of their psychic wounds to last for decades. Many of these warriors were reluctant to discuss their painful experiences in the war with anyone except fellow combat veterans. Similar to my father's experience with the Veterans Administration, many others were told by medical professionals not to complain and to just get on with their lives.[12] Even the VA Vet Centers, community mental health centers created by Congress and the Veterans Administration in 1979 to deal with the readjustment needs of the Vietnam veterans, were not open to veterans of either World War II or the Korean War until 1996, reflective of the lack of recognition of the trauma of those veterans. Roy Driver, director of a Vet Center in Lewiston, Maine, noted that elderly vets can be more difficult to help than those of the more recent wars because of the passage of time. According to Driver, the main reason these men come to the World War II groups at the vet center is to find support from each other and to know that after all these years, they are not alone in their struggle with their war memories.[13] By the end of the first decade of the twenty-first century, the VA was receiving and granting more and more first-time disability claims for stress-related reasons to veterans who were in their eighth decade of life. In the first eight years of this century, the number of WWII vets collecting benefits

11. Scott Sleek, "Older veterans just now feeling pain of war," APA Monitor 29(5) (May 1995).

12. Mark Van Ells, "Coping with the Emotional Numbing of Combat," Veterans of Foreign Wars Magazine 90, October 2002, 18–20.

13. Anthony Ronzio, "World War II vets learning to not suffer in silence," Sun Journal, November 12, 2006.

for psychological reasons rose by fifty percent, in spite of the attrition in
the total number of those vets who were dying at a rapid rate.

"We were done wrong," said one World War II veteran of the European campaign who had spent a year in a German prisoner-of-war camp.
"We didn't get what we deserved. There was no understanding of what
was going on."

When he was released from the camp, the military ordered him,
along with the other POWS, "to never talk about the horrors" because it
would be "too upsetting for the home front."

An eighty-eight-year-old veteran of Iwo Jima said, "It never goes
away . . . I have flashbacks all the time." He was finally compensated for
war stress and joined a vet center group when he was eighty-five. "The
man who didn't cry for 75 years now sheds tears every day."[14]

During recent years, clinicians have posited that the number of
World War II veterans affected with PTSD is much higher than the one
in twenty estimates provided by the VA's National Center for PTSD. The
chief of psychology at the Cleveland VA Medical Center thought that
as many as thirty percent of the combat veterans of World War II might
have been affected. Since showing symptoms of emotional distress was
a huge stigma for the warriors of that generation, we may never have an
accurate statistic for the mental toll of World War II.[15]

There is also no way to know the suicide rate of the World War II
veteran population in the decades after the war ended. Data has not been
specifically collected on that group of veterans, but there is documentation that veterans as a group have a higher rate of suicide. A twelve-year
study comparing men who had served in the military between 1917 and
1994 with men without military service found that the suicide rate for
male veterans was double that of non-veterans.[16]

An investigation into the rate of suicide among elderly World War
II veterans raises provocative questions regarding the permanence of war
trauma. This investigation by The Bay Citizen and New America Media,

14. Joe Vargo, "Still fighting war stress: VA granting more first-time disability claims to veterans in their
80s than ever before," *The Press-Enterprise*, April 13, 2008.
15. Brian Albrecht, "War's Grip on Vets: Post-traumatic stress disorder hitting World War II veterans,"
Plain Dealer, July 6, 2009.
16. Mark S. Kaplan, Nathalie Huguet, Bentson H. McFarland, and Jason Newsom, "Suicide among
male veterans: a prospective population-based study," *Journal of Epidemiology and Community Health* 61(7)
(July 2007), 619–24.

which focused on one state, showed that "there's a massive amount of pain" hidden by the reticent exterior of the Greatest Generation. "In California, World War II-era veterans are killing themselves at a rate that's nearly four times higher than that of people the same age without military service. The suicide rate among these veterans is also roughly double the rate of veterans under thirty-five who are returning home from Iraq and Afghanistan.[17]

The words of my father echo in my mind. When I asked him in his later years why he never talked about his war trauma, he told me, "No one wanted to hear about it." In 2011, the same sentiment was expressed to me during a conversation I had with an elderly World War II Navy veteran with three years of service on the USS *Ancon*, a naval command and communications ship that had been in many pivotal battles in both war theaters. "We returned home with the same problems that these young guys have coming back from Iraq and Afghanistan today. But no one cared back then."

17. Aaron Glantz, "Suicide Rates Soar among WWII Vets, Records Show," *The Bay Citizen*, November 11, 2010.

Carol and Dutch in California during the 1990s.

Dutch, Carol and Rosemary Vento in the 1990s.

10

I THOUGHT I WAS THE ONLY ONE

I see you've found a box of my things -
Infantries, tanks and smoldering airplane wings.
These old pictures are cool. Tell me some stories.
Was it like the old war movies?
Sit down, son. Let me fill you in.

Where to begin? Let's start with the end.
This black-and-white photo don't capture the skin.
From the flash of a gun to a soldier who's done,
Trust me, grandson,
The war was in color.

From shipyard to sea, From factory to sky,
From rivet to rifle, from boot camp to battle cry,
I wore the mask up high on a daylight run,
That held my face in its clammy hand,
Crawled over coconut logs and corpses in the coral sand.

Where to begin? Let's start with the end.
This black-and-white photo don't capture the skin.
From the shock of a shell or the memory of smell,
If red is for Hell,
The war was in color.

—"The War Was in Color" by Carbon Leaf

"Friendship is born at that moment when one person says to another:
'What! You too? I thought I was the only one'."

—C.S. Lewis

From the perspective of their Baby Boomer children, the Greatest Generation should have been called the Silent Generation. I had read the books, viewed the documentaries, and watched The Longest Day a dozen times. From these sources, I have gained more knowledge of my father's participation in World War II than most other progeny of veterans. Knowing the details of Dad's war made me proud, but my feelings about the "good war" were complicated. I was impressed by my Dad's bravery and resilience and grateful that he had survived horrendous battles where so many men had perished, but I had the sense, unarticulated and not fully understood for a long time, that my father had not escaped World War II unscathed. My book knowledge of Normandy, Market Garden and the Bulge did not help me comprehend the existence or persistence of Dad's invisible wounds. And I certainly thought that my father's reaction to the war and the impact on our family was somewhat unique. After all, the narrative was that all the other men who came home from the war in Europe and the Pacific raised happy, well-adjusted children and rebuilt America into a world power. It appeared to me that the Schultz family was an anomaly.

It wasn't until Ilene Baker and I, first colleagues at work and then friends, started talking about our D-Day fathers that we both realized there was a hidden story lurking behind the façade of our fearless fathers, which impacted the psyche of some children of Greatest Generation warriors. When Ilene accompanied me on the trip to California to say goodbye to my dying father, we realized that our shared experience was broader than we had thought. Ilene was able to print out a page which heralded our new website, Daughters of D-Day, and show it to my Dad. Even though he was in his last weeks of life, Dad was able to respond emphatically, "Tell your stories—that's what's important now. So many of the veterans' stories have been told. Let people know what it was like to have a father who had been in the war."

After Dad died, we fleshed out our site more and asked for stories, not only from other daughters, not only from children of D-Day veterans but from all children of World War II, with an emphasis on those whose fathers and relatives had been in combat zones. As Ilene Baker so aptly put it in our mission statement on the site:

There seems to be some unspoken connection that the children of World War II veterans shared . . . It seemed clear to us that the men who served in combat must have returned home from war in a traumatized state, and it was something that no one was prepared to deal with at that time . . . The great anguish that these men, our fathers, carried home with them is mirrored in the 'collective unconscious wound' that we, as their adult children, now need to confront.[1]

As we began to receive comments and stories, we realized that we were right. We were not alone in wondering and reflecting on the impact of World War II and its aftermath on our lives. Possibly as a reflection of their fathers' silence and shame, a number of poignant comments and emails were anonymous. The emotional toll of war had not been spoken of when Baby Boomers were young, and it still seemed to be a source of shame for the now-adult children of the warriors.

In 2007, Ken Burns' documentary, *The War*, occasioned some discussion of the psychological cost to World War II veterans. I called into an NPR show on this topic and told of our website. This comment was posted on our Daughters of D-Day blog the next day:

I listened to a discussion with Carol on public radio when she talked about her father . . . For myself, my father fought in WWII and stayed in the military . . . while in the Army, he suffered psychiatric breakdowns (1954-55) that sent him into Walter Reed twice, where he was treated as a nutcase rather than someone suffering from PTSD . . . Rather than discharge him they kept him in the Army. In 1957, just before his 37th birthday, he committed suicide. I was 10 . . . So yes, I am a Daughter of D-Day. That day was probably the happiest day my father ever had. In a few short years, he was already a dead man, even if he did not physically die on some field in Europe.[2]

---

1. Ilene Baker, Daughters of D-Day website, http://daughtersofd-day.com/daughters.htm.
2. Daughters of D-Day blog, http://daughtersofd-day.blogspot.com.

I created another blog, *Legacy of War*, which dealt more specifically with the psychological issues of World War II and received more sad and telling anonymous comments:

> My father was distant and always worried about something. He never talked about the war, just a short story to explain the horrible scar on his back . . . It did not dawn on me until about 3-4 years ago that he had PTSD . . . I've had to work through some pretty dysfunctional problems and still have some panic issues, but at least now I kind of know the root of them.

Another Legacy of War post told of a daughter realizing the fear of lobotomy that her father spoke about when he was in a VA hospital was not a delusion. Her father had been in a VA hospital neuropsychiatric unit shortly after the war ended and was diagnosed with one of the catchall terms of the time: "psychopathological personality–mixed." The daughter, who dubbed herself Daddy's POW, researched information about her father and his hospital.

> She was enlightened in a way she did not expect—the background . . . included information about the lobotomies performed there. Would you seek mental health treatment if you thought there was a chance you might be lobotomized?

Another daughter shared, on the *Legacy of War*, the thoughts she had when she visited the National D-Day Memorial located in Bedford, Virginia, the American town which suffered the highest per capita D-Day losses when the 29th Infantry Division went ashore on Omaha Beach in the first wave. She reflected on her father:

> My father fought in this war. He did not triumph over his demons, and upon my birth, I became a casualty of war. I know little about him . . . He was a handsome, put-together man when I met him on rare occasions. My childhood memories of his trips included chips, soda, and ice cream. They are mingled with the adult knowledge of his alcoholism and drug

addictions. I can't escape the visual picture of the disfiguring surgery on his face, which rendered him unable to eat and speak. Too much drink combined with too much smoking made him one of the five men who had the same disfiguring surgery in a VA hospital in Connecticut on the same day.

Many World War II veterans, my father included, told their children the funny stories of being in the war. Another Legacy of War comment mirrored the experience of many of us:

> My Dad glorified his WWII service as all making whiskey, drinking whiskey, stealing jeeps from the other services and general fun times. Then we got older, and some of the truth came out . . . After he died, we found letters to my mother about his waking from nightmares after returning from the Pacific. He was a lawyer with an undergrad in psychology, but he drank himself to an early death.

The reality that war was not all fun and games came late to most, as another daughter noted in 2009:

> I grew up listening to my Dad and uncles' war stories, never realizing the silent demons that drove my Dad's chaotic behavior and made my life . . . a living hell. We found out a few years ago that Dad (still living) . . . suffers from PTSD . . . It blows my mind that I wasn't even born when my Dad was fighting in the Philippines, and now . . . the effect of WWII is still living on in me.

An email we received at our *Daughters of D-Day* website described what the author's father did not talk about to her:

> He did come home from the war in 1946 after serving with the 504th Parachute Infantry Regiment. He married my mother right away and never talked much about the war. But his drinking became a problem early in the marriage, and by the time I

was born, the fourth child in that troubled marriage, he was an alcoholic. He died a lonely death by an accidental fire in 1964.

This daughter has spent the last twenty years of her own life burrowing into the limited information she was able to obtain about her father's war, attempting to understand how her father's demons had impacted her.

Anonymous postings and emails are but a sampling of the dialogue we have had with other children of World War II veterans.[3] When we have given presentations in various settings, there are always children and veterans who come up after, not asking public questions but wanting us to know that our experiences mirror their own and thanking us for talking publicly about it. Ilene and I both have friends who do not want to share their upbringings and relationships with their fathers publicly but have talked to us about the troubled past within their families.

A male friend of mine, who does not wish to be identified, permitted me to share the story of his World War II Marine veteran father. Often, sons of World War II veterans had rocky relationships with their Dads, as illustrated in Tom Mathews' book *Our Fathers' War: Growing Up in the Shadow of the Greatest Generation.* Many combat veterans of that era expected their sons to be tough and would not tolerate any signs of what they considered to be softness. This take-no-prisoners technique, according to Mathews, caused significant generational strife. My friend, who I am identifying as J, had a similar experience with his father. J's father was a Harvard graduate when he enlisted in the Marines. He saw fierce fighting in the Pacific, including Iwo Jima and Okinawa. During the latter battle, he was seriously wounded. Fellow Marines dragged him out of a cave to receive medical attention. He received two Purple Hearts and the Bronze Star and was proud of his war record. As a young boy, J idolized his Marine father and often dressed up in Dad's uniform and played with war paraphernalia. During J's teenage years, the relationship became complicated. His father had become a functioning alcoholic and was often abusive towards his son, telling him he was "making a man out of him." J left home at 18 and never returned. From J's perspective, the war negatively impacted his family life. J's mother was the daughter

---

3. Legacy of War blog, http://www.dutchschultz.blogspot.com.

of a World War II admiral. When she married J's father, her image of her husband was of the handsome Marine hero. J's father did not have a successful career, and his wife berated him for his failures. He never lived up to that hero persona in her eyes. J's father rarely discussed the war, except for the occasional humorous stories, but in a rare moment of truth-telling, J's father confided in his son his feeling of failing his fellow Marines when he was wounded and had to leave them.[4]

Some daughters have wanted to share more details about the impact of World War II. Like Ilene and I, it often took much of their adult life for them to understand that the war did not end when the fighting was over.

Like me, Lorinda Pate is the daughter of a paratrooper. Daughters of hardened combat veterans may have been treated more gently than sons, but not by much. Lorinda and I had similar upbringings, being taught by their paratrooper Dads never to walk away from a fight, to stand your ground. Albert Anthony Pate was a rifleman and paratrooper with the 551st Parachute Infantry Division, a unit which was dissolved after World War II and absorbed into the 82nd Airborne. The 551st fought in Italy, France, and Belgium, where they were almost decimated, suffering an eighty-five percent casualty rate. Because of the inactivation of the unit, their bravery was not recognized for years. Gregory Oraflea, a son of one of the paratroopers from the 551st, wrote *Messengers of the Lost Battalion,* and its publication in 1997 filled in many of the blanks about the neglected heroism of the 551st. Albert Pate was one of the survivors of that unit, a unit where so many brave men were lost. Lorinda remembers her childhood as one in which she felt loved by her Dad, who did his best to make her "tough."

Lorinda described her father:

Dad was absolutely fearless . . . His tongue was a horsewhip, his knuckles were brass, but his heart was pure gold. He had no patience for fools and could be cruel in his admonishments, but there was nothing he would not do for his friends and family.

He taught me to shoot and taught me to fight, trying his best to

4. J, Interview by author, August 2005.

make me tough, but I could never come close to measuring up to him.

In watching the movie "Patton," where the General becomes enraged at the whimpering soldier who is in the field hospital claiming "battle fatigue," I saw my father mirrored in Patton's actions. As the General smacked the cowering soldier and ordered him back to the front lines, I saw my father berating me when I would come home crushed by the taunts of schoolyard bullies and neighborhood kids who would steal my toys.

While I was growing up, Dad was the original, "You'd better stop crying, or I'll give you something to cry about," man. No tears were allowed! He taught me to fight "like a man" using Army combat moves. "First, go for the face, but kick to the stomach instead; then, when he doubles over, clamp your hands together and crack him behind the head to bring him to the ground, a swift kick or two to teach him respect, then take your toys and walk . . . don't run . . . home (all the while watching behind you for retaliation). Never show fear."

Well, the battle-honed rage that enabled my father to charge through enemy lines, slashing blindly through forest and flesh, came alive in me during my childhood tussles. I still remember the terrifying madness that blocked out my consciousness and made me oblivious to the pain being inflicted upon me by my foe. I came back to reality as my screaming 6th-grade teacher pulled me off the much larger boy whose head I was repeatedly bashing into the asphalt of the playground. "Stop, you're killing him!" It was frightening, that murderous rage. My father was so proud when the Principal called him to come take me home.

Lorinda has childhood memories of her father's PTSD, not fully comprehending at the time why he slept with a dagger under his pillow or why he was always sad at Christmas. According to oldtimers who knew Albert before the war, he came home only with frostbitten feet, as lucky on the battlefield as he had been in the gambling saloons of his hometown, Weirton, West Virginia. Albert's younger sister remembered his homecoming as being more troubled—at night, he would kick,

scream and pound the wall in his bedroom. The war had not yet left
Albert when Lorinda was young:

> I vividly remember an incident that occurred when I was about
> 4 or 5 years old . . . Getting up to use the bathroom late one
> night as a small child will, I stepped into the hall, and before I
> could reach the light switch, I came face to face with a monster!
> I screamed . . . It was my father, crouched down with a huge
> Army dagger at ready. Needless to say, I never got up in the
> middle of the night again!
>
> Christmas was always less than Merry. Not for lack of pres-
> ents, of which there were many, but because of some mysterious
> "Battle of the Bulge" that my father always brought up again
> and again when Mom tried in vain to get him to join in festivi-
> ties with other relatives. He'd go out to a bar, and we wouldn't
> see him until the celebrations were over. Coincidentally, my
> father died on the anniversary of the Malmedy Massacre, during
> the season of the Battle of the Bulge, and alas . . . Christmas.
>
> It was many years, books and movies later, before I realized
> how horrific Dad's WWII experiences were . . . Having to gut
> young German soldiers like one would gut a fish, using dagger,
> bayonet and rifle-butt while his adversaries pleaded for mercy.
> He fought his foes face to face. He wasn't firing at abstract mov-
> ing objects on a far-away atoll, or at a target viewed through
> a ship's torpedo sight, or shooting from an airplane flying
> overhead. It was hand to hand; German blood mingled with his
> own. Dad kept the ID photos . . . Hundreds of them. He told
> me later that some of the dying Germans had begged him to
> give their loved ones a message once the war was over. I don't
> know if he ever delivered the soldier's messages, but I found
> letters in German among his effects.

Many moves occurred during Lorinda's young years, with her father
working construction, continuing his gambling and drinking. Her parents divorced but always remained friends, and neither remarried, although her father always had a woman in tow. When Albert talked about

the war, he would laughingly recount dancing through the minefields in France with wine bottles pilfered from a chateau clinking in his knapsack. It wasn't until after her father's death that Lorinda found medals, commendations, photos and other war memorabilia among his effects. He died just as he lived, "ready to walk off the battlefield . . . Triumphant and without fear." And Lorinda, like so many daughters of World War II combat vets, was left to grieve the man who had had such an influence on the type of woman she became.

> I never for one moment wished that I had been raised by a more gentle man. My father's cynical views on life, coupled with his determination to wring every bit of pleasure from this earthly existence, remind me of his dancing through the minefields . . . wine bottles clinking merrily in his knapsack. Knowing full well that at any moment, he could be blown to bits, he forged ahead regardless, finding some small burst of joy in even the most harrowing experience. Now, I'm left to navigate life's minefields alone, wine bottles clinking as I attempt to dance.[5]

Baby Boomers are the first group which comes to mind when the children of World War II veterans are mentioned. After all, we were 75 million strong. It is not known how many of the group born between 1946 and 1964 were progeny of World War II veterans, but tens of millions must have been, just based on the sheer number of men—16.2 million—who were in the military during the war. Little known or recognized is that many men were already fathers when they left their homes for the war effort. Approximately 183,000 American children lost their fathers to the war. Nayda's father did return home, but he was a changed man.

Nayda Colomb was born in 1939 and was not yet three years old when her thirty-four-year-old father enlisted in the Army in September of 1942. Basic training was at Fort Knox, Kentucky, and soon, this mature, intelligent man was sent to Officer Candidate School. Besides Nayda, he had left behind his wife, two other children, and a career as a pharmaceutical salesman. The family moved to Indiana to be closer to

---

5. Unpublished essay, Lorinda Pate, "Dancing through the Minefields" (March 2006).

their maternal grandparents while they waited for their breadwinner to come home. Nayda described what she knows of her father's arrival in Europe in the summer of 1944:

> My father joined the Seventh Armored Division in Belgium in the summer of 1944. He found the time in a replacement unit in England "interesting," for he was curious about the place and people, much as a tourist would be. He arrived on Omaha Beach and went through Paris to meet his unit after the city was liberated, feeling like a hero as the French greeted him and his buddies. Needless to say, the idea of tourist and hero was soon dispelled by the brutal cold of that winter and the return of the Germans in the Battle of the Bulge.
>
> I can scarcely comprehend the idea that within two weeks of arriving in the Ardennes, he became company commander for his tank unit. This was the result of the high loss of life among the Seventh in previous battles, as well as his rank and maturity. In speaking with his gunner in recent years, I asked how it was for guys like him, who had been in the unit through many battles in the past two years, to take orders from one who had no experience. He said it wasn't always easy, for they knew some decisions were not wise, yet they couldn't say anything. He also said they called my Dad "Pops" behind his back due to his age—at thirty-five!
>
> Intense fighting was the order of the day for these men as they tried to push the Germans back across the line and hold them. Our men were ill-equipped for the harsh winter, and at one point, Dad said he had on everything he owned in an attempt to keep warm. He had pneumonia soon upon arrival and was briefly hospitalized before returning to his unit. The fierce battles of December 16-18th in the area of St. Vith challenged him and earned him a Silver Star for his work against great opposition. He was later to receive a Purple Heart due to a shrapnel injury. Suffice it to say, he was a true "combat veteran" in early 1945 and crossed the Rhine Bridge at Remagen into

Germany with great satisfaction. By August of 1945, he had enough points to return home from Berlin.

Nayda was five when her father returned from war–old enough to remember family life upon his homecoming. During the early years after the war, the family was readjusting. Her father resumed his career as a pharmaceutical salesman, and they all returned to Ohio. However, the stress level increased with time.

I have two memories that indicate the stress level of the household during this time. Our family was having dinner prior to attending an evening event at school. We were having roast beef, mashed potatoes and gravy. I was sitting beside Dad, and he began to ladle gravy on my plate when I pushed the gravy bowl away, for I didn't like gravy. The extremely hot liquid spilled onto my hand and burned it badly. He is the one who helped clean it off and attended to the burns and bandages. I don't believe we made it to school that evening. I recall very few times when he attended school functions, for he smoked and drank and couldn't do that while at school. The second memory is of coming home for dinner after playing outside. I had a sweater when I left home but had taken it off. I didn't have it when I returned home. It was autumn, and got dark early. When he asked me about the sweater, and I said I didn't know where it was, he gruffly told me to go outside and not come back until I had found it. You can imagine my fear as I searched the area around the house, hoping I could soon be back where it was warm and light!

Ensuing years brought a succession of moves with different houses and jobs. Dad was a successful salesman and seemed always to be looking for the next opportunity. He began his own pharmaceutical company in about 1948. It was a very stressful time for each of us. I believe this is the period when he was combining alcohol and Phenobarbitol, for he had free access. I also recall his frustration with owning his own business, and he threatened to "burn the damn thing down." He finally sold it to an established company and became a sales manager for them. This led to a succession of moves in this position, with the explanation that he would establish a successful sales force and then want the challenge of another business that was not doing well. I have a letter from a friend who worked with him indicating he was terminated in one of the companies. I can only speculate as to the reason . . . these were years of great turmoil in our home, with arguing and some physical violence, as well as one incident when Dad got into the car and left late in the night. He was drinking as usual, and I recall sitting on the closed stairs to the kitchen with my sister, crying due to the things I heard and fearing for Dad's safety driving while angry and drunk.

Clearly, he drank regularly. If he didn't return from work before five-thirty, I knew he had stopped at the American Legion for "a drink," and dinner would be late when he arrived, inebriated. I grew more tense as the hours wore on, and my evening was not a happy one. Many times during high school years this habit dominated our household and kept my sister and me from participating in some school functions, for dinner was too late and at an unpredictable time.

Nayda married young, at nineteen, to escape the tension in her family home. Her husband was eight years older than her. After her children were grown, she knew that her deteriorating first marriage was taking a toll on her physical and emotional health. She began attending Adult Children of Alcoholic (ACOA) meetings:

It was quite a shock to read that first book and realize I shared many characteristics common to children of alcoholics. Part of me was relieved. Another part of me felt "robbed" of being a unique personality. I did find fellowship and understanding among those attending meetings. I felt heard and understood by them, something I needed badly. I had several close friends who also provided this support during the difficult years.

Yes, my life has definitely been affected by my father's years of combat in WWII. My self-esteem and trust suffered badly, causing some decisions that were unwise, particularly in the choice of a marriage partner. I began to say my spouse was "all of the things Dad was not and none of the things he was." I respected my father more in spite of his weaknesses than I did my spouse. I felt more loved by my father, yet I hadn't learned to appreciate my own gifts from either relationship. As a teacher, I grew stronger in self-esteem and gradually understood how self-deprecating I had been. My students, their parents and my co-workers respected and appreciated me for who I was.

Nayda's father's war caught up with him when he was fifty-eight. At that time, he was the Executive Director of the American Cancer Society in Dayton, Ohio. His health quickly went downhill:

He lost the ability to do this work and declined rapidly into a state of hallucination and senility, no longer able to dress or feed himself or find his way to the bathroom. He was admitted to the VA Hospital in Marion, Indiana, at the age of sixty-one and died there at sixty-five. He was never ambulatory during that time and didn't recognize anyone or anything. We are grateful for the excellent care he received while there, relieving our mother of caring for him twenty-four hours a day. Clearly, he did suffer the effects of the battlefield and the things he witnessed in the Ardennes Forest and Bergen Belsen. Each of our family members also experienced the result of his wartime service, followed by alcohol and drug addiction. The results remain with us today in ourselves as well as our children and grandchildren. Understanding is one way of intercepting this cycle through the generations.

Similar to many of the adult children who have reflected on their families, Nayda was able to understand the struggles and look back with compassion.

I can only speculate as to the ways each of our lives would have been different if he had not seen combat. I know we would still have challenges, and alcoholism may have been one of them. I am grateful for the family I had, for I felt loved and was able to love and accept my parents in spite of the emotional turmoil in our household. I feel gratitude for the fact that my father was an intelligent, gregarious person who was assertive and succeeded in his career. He and I are both "Lifetime Learners," and I treasure this trait. More than anger, I feel sadness for the lives of my family, which were less fulfilling than they may have been and grateful for the life I have.[6]

Nanette Arndts is unique, not only because she is the child of a World War II veteran of the Pacific and a Holocaust survivor, but also through her method of expression. *The Philadelphia Inquirer* magazine called her a belter of the blues "whose soul fights its way out and fills the room with well-seasoned wisdom and joy." Known as Sister Blue, this Philly native fronts a blues band. *Northeast Times'* Jim Albert says that "no one, not even Mick Jagger in Tina Turner's body, can move onstage like Sister Blue."[7]

Leonard Goldman, Nanette's father, is her role model. He was the parent who raised Nanette and her brother after their parents divorced. Leonard was inducted into the Army in June 1943 and did not return to Philadelphia until January 1946. Nanette recounts her father's service:

My father finally arrived in the Pacific, where he served in three combat zones. Initially, he served in New Caledonia, then in the Philippines. In Guadalcanal, my father served as security after the enormous battle there, which he remembers as the most frightening place he was stationed, enduring much gunfire. My father was stationed in Bougainville, Green Island, and Leyte. And he was in the anti-aircraft division, where all the guys contracted dysentery. My father was then aboard the *Hokeida*, a cargo ship headed for Japan. In contrast to the

---

6. Unpublished essay, Nayda Colomb, "My Father, Myself" (August 2011).
7. Sister Blue, www.sisterblueband.com.

boiling 100-degree-plus temperatures at night on the islands, the soldiers found themselves riding in open jeeps in the frigid snow when they arrived in Japan. This dramatic weather change resulted in most of the men going to sick bay. My father was stationed in Otou, then Sepura, until the end of the war, and he recalls all the ships lighting up when the war was over. He stayed in Japan for six weeks as an MP (military police), at the end of the war.

Leonard's stories about the war were mainly humorous, and while he never spoke of the horrors of war, he told Nanette he had friends who lost their lives. He served in New Caledonia, the Philippines and Guadalcanal, both in anti-aircraft and security divisions. Leonard was the steady parent and appeared not to carry the trauma of war home with him. Nanette's mother had a more difficult time.

My mother surviving Nazi Germany affected me in a more negative way. She was born in Cologne, Germany, to Jewish Polish immigrants, making my mother, according to German law, a Polish citizen. After Kristallnacht, it was illegal for my mother and her family to be alive. Many family members on my mother's side perished in the Holocaust. Her pain, which I'm told is unique to children of survivors, sometimes manifested itself into a rage, which I know resolves nothing, resulting in no healing.

My mother survived in Belgium, where she suffered intense fear during the Battle of the Bulge. She was told when the whistling of the bombs stopped, that was when it was dangerous. My mother had the frightening experience of a bomb dropping too close. Here she was liberated, and she feared the Nazis would rule Belgium once again. Thanks to the courage of our men, the Americans prevailed, for which I feel eternally grateful. Were it not for these men, my existence, that of my children and future generations, would be questionable. On a lighter note, my mother, being a young woman, recalls how she knew which soldiers were the Americans because they tucked their pants into their boots, and my mother found that "so sexy." My mother's visa was stamped Belgium, and she arrived in the United States in 1948. My mother became a citizen in 1960 after being married to my father in 1956.

Nanette considers herself a true child of World War II. Both her parents survived the war on different continents:[8]

Ultimately, both of my parents made me more grateful than most Americans. I realize just how lucky I am to be an American, not only by choice but also by birthright. As a nation, we may have made terrible judgments, but we, as common people, can make change. Even though we may passionately disagree with our fellow Americans or our administration, we have the right to candidly voice our argument, thanks to the bravery and courage of the soldiers of World War II, like my father.

Ilene Baker, the co-creator of *Daughters of D-Day* and my friend and colleague, always knew her World War II father, Joe Baker, was in Normandy and always knew she was adopted. What she did not know was how the intersection of war and adoption would influence her decades later. When Ilene and I created our website in 2005, she pulled out a box of photographs and war memorabilia she had kept on a shelf in her home after the death of her parents. Her father, Joe, did not bring home any overt symptoms of war trauma, but Ilene sensed that the war nonetheless impacted him deeply. One photograph, in particular, intrigued her. It was a young boy, possibly about thirteen. Her elderly paternal aunt had recently mentioned that Joe had wanted to adopt a young French boy during the war. Could this be the boy in the photo? Ilene began to investigate:

I had hit a dead end. I went back to the box of photographs, looking for something that might give me a clue to help me. I found it. There was one photograph of a destroyed plane on a beach of sorts, with homes in the background. The text on the

---

8. Unpublished essay, Nanette Arndts, "My Father, My Hero, My Friend" (April 2006).

back said: "Part of an American airplane shot down on one of the Islands. Some fishermen's homes. Some boats, when the tide is down and part of a fish net. Where I am standing is underwater when the tide is in." I had found the connection. On the web there are so very many sites that digging through them is truly like looking for the proverbial needle in a haystack. After some searching, I found that there was a bomber named the *Daisey Mae Scraggs* that had been shot down two days after D-Day over a small island named Chausey . . .

I compared my father's photograph of the downed plane with one that I found on a website called *Le Iles Chausey*. They were almost identical. A new round of emails began . . . Several weeks after this flurry of emails, I received an email from one of the contacts by the name of Hervé Hillard saying:

Sorry for this late answer, but I first thought your mail was some sort of a joke. In fact, the little boy in the pictures is one of my friends' father! His name was Jean Thévenin (my friend's name is Jean-Michel). Jean Thévenin became a Chausey fisherman, got married and had two boys, Jean-Michel and Stéphane, and died about 20 years ago. I've the professional email of Jean-Michel. The best would be to write him directly because he has thousands of questions to ask you! Thanks by advance. It's quite an incredible story, and I do hope we'll all get all the answers we're looking for!

It didn't seem real to me. I had located the child. I was sad that I wouldn't be able to tell the boy grown into a man that my father had saved photographs of him until his death, nor would I be able to ask the questions that I hoped to get answers to, but it really was enough to be able to give a name to the child with the bright eyes in the picture.

And the same photograph was in the home of the son of the boy in the picture:

So, it seems as if the photograph of the boy that my father saved for 55 years, until his death, was also saved by said boy, Jean

Thévenin, until his death, and now it was up to me to discover why.

Ilene began a correspondence with Jean Michel, the son of Jean Thevenin, and eventually visited him in Chausey. She found out more about her father's war and the circumstances that brought Ilene and Jean Michel together decades later.[9]

Eddie Livingston was a decorated World War II 82nd Airborne paratrooper and pathfinder. Among his medals and awards were a Distinguished Service Cross, three Bronze Stars and seven Purple Hearts. Eddie was also a prisoner of war, held captive by the Germans and forced to be on a clean-up crew in Belsen Buchenwald after the killings in that horrific concentration camp. Eddie survived, haunted by battle memories and struggled with the Veterans Administration for decades trying to get help for his war trauma. Eddie lived with his wife for thirty years in a small house in Alabama with no running water or electricity. Pam Baker, his niece, shared her home in California with Eddie during the final years of his life. After his death, Pam arranged for Eddie's ashes to be carried eastward toward Alabama by the Patriot Guard and Run for the Wall motorcycle riders. Pam wanted the tribute and honor not received in life paid to Eddie in death. Pam continues to create a legacy, posting many letters and essays by Eddie, a prolific and gifted writer. Eddie articulated for years his frustration about how the invisible wounds suffered by combat veterans of World War II were ignored. Eddie's bravery in the early morning hours of D-Day, setting up drop zones prior to the main paratrooper drop, is portrayed in a 2011 film, *Pathfinders: In the Company of Strangers*.[10]

Each of us has a story, different but connected in some way. Our fathers and uncles often returned from war as different men, and their changes influenced the direction of our lives. Some of us lived through family struggles. Some upbringings were more peaceful. But the common thread is what we didn't know about the hidden legacy of World War II.

---

9. Ilene Baker, "The Time of High Tide," *N4Normandy: The Anglo Magazine for Normandy* (March 2010), accessed August 10, 2011, http://magazinenfornormandy.com/2010/03/hightide4/.

10. Pam Baker, Facebook Page, http://facebook.com/pambaker3.

Albert and Lorinda Pate.

Nanette and Jordan Arndts with Leonard Goldman.

Nanette Arndts, Sister Blue.

Nayda Swonger Colomb and father.

Ilene and Joe Baker.

11

CONCLUSION

"Talk to the children" was the directive from the unshaven, emaciated man. As he lay dying, the old master sergeant issued his last order to me. The end was nearing on my complicated relationship with my paratrooper Dad.

I have experienced the Greatest Generation story from both sides. My Navy veteran stepfather has been a rock of stability for me over the thirty years he has been in my life. My paratrooper father, who taught me valuable life lessons of persistence in the face of major odds and obstacles, set a template for my successful development into adulthood. Since Dad was plucked from obscurity in 1959 by Cornelius Ryan, I have been given a vantage point at the intersection of myth, history and reality not available to many of the children of World War II veterans.

Lee Bondy's war experience, not specifically and individually highlighted in military history books, is part of the combat history of the Pacific. The *Cleveland* was engaged in major naval battles. Even though he was in a combat zone, Lee did not return home with war trauma and personifies more accurately the Greatest Generation narrative.

In the twenty-first century, with another generation that has returned from the wars in Afghanistan and Iraq, there is an ongoing debate about what predisposes a warrior to post-traumatic stress disorder. I certainly do not have the answer. I am well aware that not every combat veteran struggles after their return. But many do, and the story of their struggle should be included in what the public knows about the Greatest Generation.

Pieces of Arthur 'Dutch' Schultz's war were first known to World War II buffs in Ryan's *Longest Day* and two following books, *A Bridge Too Far* and *The Last Battle*. With the renewed interest in the war in the nineteen

nineties, a new generation of authors sought out my Dad for a retelling
of his stories. The new flood of books at the end of the twentieth century
portrayed my Dad and others as war heroes. While my father appreciated
the recognition, he did not feel he was worthy of the title of hero. Not
feeling that he did more than any other combat soldier, Dad said the
real heroes never returned home. Dad minimized his bravery, even while
others lauded it. He knew all too well the limitations of the Greatest
Generation myth and the personal cost to him and others. My father
never hid his postwar struggles, but that part of his story was not of much
interest to military historians. Except for a brief mention in Ed Ruggero's
book, *The First Men In: U.S. Paratroopers and the Fight to Save D-Day*,
Dad's problems after the war were never mentioned. He told Ruggero, as
he had said to other authors, that his return was difficult. "Later, Schultz
had some difficulties of his own . . . descended into alcoholism, losing
his career and his family."[1]

Even though I found letters from my father to the authors in the
Ryan and Ambrose archives telling of his difficult reentry, these types of
stories, which did not fit into the accepted storyline of the well-adjusted
World War II veterans, were not given much visibility. Books by his-
torians such as Thomas Childers' *Soldier From the War Returning: The
Troubled Homecoming of the Greatest Generation* have not taken root in
the public consciousness enough to puncture the image of the Brokaw/
Ambrose stereotype.

Kenneth Rose's *Myth and the Greatest Generation* posits that as we
move further away in time from World War II, "the shadows that obscure
this event and its impact on the lives of Americans have lengthened, and
in the process, the horrors of the battlefield have been sanitized."[2] For
those men who saw the most action on the battlefield, "it was a horror, a
stark reality largely lost to Americans in recent years."[3] The gulf between
the reality of the minority of veterans who had been in combat and the
majority who were not battle-exposed was large, according to Rose. But

---

1. Ed Ruggero, *The First Men In: U.S. Paratroopers and the Fight to Save D-Day* (New York: Harper
Collins, 2006), 304.
2. Kenneth Rose, *Myth and the Greatest Generation* (New York: Routledge—Taylor & Francis Group,
2008), 1.
3. Rose, 5.

it is the experience of that majority that has informed our collective understanding of the war.

In his sardonically titled book, *The Best War Ever*, and in a related article, Michael C.C. Adams calls the popular history of postwar World War II incomplete. "We should remember that only a small minority of soldiers saw sustained front-line combat . . . Veterans who were not in combat will tend to romanticize the memory of service more than those who were. We must listen to those who lived in the killing fields, including Joseph Heller and Kurt Vonnegut, Jr."[4]

To the list of World War II battle-scarred veterans who were noted authors should also be added Norman Mailer, James Jones, and J.D. Salinger. None of these combat-hardened men painted an idyllic picture of their time in the military, but their bestselling books were considered fiction, not based in reality.

Edward Wood, Jr. is a nonfiction writer who knows the reality of combat. A retired city planner who was severely wounded in World War II, he is cynical about what he considers the "falsification of memory" about the war. In 2006, he revealed that he struggled for most of his life with PTSD, although he managed it and was able to function well. But it was "always there, burned in the psyche, ready to attack when the right trigger is squeezed." His attempt at psychiatric help shortly after the war paralleled my father's, with Wood being told that his despair was because of his "mother, father, the Oedipus tragedy."[5]

A possible explanation for the failure of the reality of World War II to be understood by the American public might lie in censorship and the lack of information given during and after that war. Even the iconic symbol of the flag raising at Iwo Jima, a picture of determination that was a template for a photo of 9/11 terror attack responders, does not give a hint of the reality that befell most of the six Marines in that photo—three dead within a month, and two others with a sad postwar tale. News information during World War II was heavily controlled and limited. It wasn't until the springtime of 1945 that the American public saw a photo of a dead American soldier with a pool of blood next to him. Robert

4. Michael C.C. Adams, "The 'Good War' Myth and the Cult of Nostalgia," *The Midwest Quarterly* 40.1 (Autumn 1998), 59–74.

5. Edward W. Wood, Jr, *Worshiping the Myths of World War II: Reflections of America's Dedication to War* (Dulles, VA: Potomac Books, 2006), 56, 58.

Capa's picture of a GI in Leipzig, killed by a German sniper, appeared in *Life* magazine towards the end of the war in Europe. It was the first "bloody death" of World War II allowed in the press. From late 1943, more restrained photos of dead soldiers had been published, but the horror of bloodshed had not been portrayed. The Office of War Information and the Office of Censorship also kept pictures of shell-shocked soldiers out of the public eye. "Censorship and customary practice kept one particular consequence of war out of view for the duration—crying." Because the visuals of World War II were so limited, the complexity of that war was not fully understood. World War II was not on the television, being viewed in the living rooms of Americans. Unlike the Vietnam War, where soldiers' deaths were on the evening news, World War II does not have the pictorial representation of violence associated with it.[6]

For decades after World War II, the psychological breakdown of American soldiers was hidden. In John Huston's 1946 film, *Let There Be Light,* seventy-five veterans were filmed in a Long Island, New York psychiatric hospital undergoing treatment for their war trauma. Not until 1981 was there a public viewing of the film. "In the late 40s, the Army seemed to feel that the film would scare off potential recruits. In his 1994 autobiography, *An Open Book,* Mr. Huston reports the Army justified its censorship on the grounds that a public showing of the film would invade the privacy of the soldiers."[7]

Not only were photographs and films about death, blood, and psychological trauma relating to World War II kept from the public, but experiments that were being performed on American soldiers were also hidden. Mustard gas experiments were done to investigate whether exposure to the gas would affect soldiers of different races differently. The Office of Scientific Research and Development designed these experiments to determine how effective protective clothing, ointments, or gas masks would be in protecting soldiers. The young men were encouraged to "volunteer" with messages of patriotic duty and promises of extra pay and leave privileges. The pain caused by the intentional application or spraying of mustard gas ranged from skin burns and blistering to eye

---

6. George H. Roeder, Jr., *The Censored War: America's Visual Experience During World War Two* (New Haven, CT: Yale University Press, 1993), 1, 3, 124.

7. Vincent Canby, "'Let There Be Light,' John Huston vs. the Army," *New York Times,* 16 January 1981.

injuries and lung damage. Some men who had been placed in gas cham-
bers reported feelings of intense fear. Four of the research projects were
conducted at Cornell and the University of Chicago in addition to other
sites. Reports note that there were "at least four research projects that
compared mustard gas exposure in African American soldiers to white
soldiers, and at least four projects that compared Japanese American soldiers to white soldiers." The San Jose project, conducted on an island
near Panama, was designed to compare the responses of Puerto Rican soldiers with Caucasian soldiers after exposure to mustard gas. The results
of these tests were not conclusive, with preliminary results suggesting
African Americans were more resistant to mustard gas being dismissed
for insufficient testing. According to the study directors, "There do not
appear to have been . . . gas chamber . . . tests to determine whether the
casualty-producing effect of . . . mustard gas in Negroes . . . is sufficiently
less than that of whites to be of practical significance in wartime." Over-
all, the study conclusions did not give much information about race.[8]

These experiments, which seemed like science fiction, unfortunately,
were real. Just as the American public had no clue that lobotomies were
being performed on veterans as part of cooperative studies and experiments, there was also no knowledge of the mustard gas trials. The ghastly
nature of these studies led to a ban. In 1953, based on the Nuremberg
Code, the Army presented guidelines for research with chemical agents,
and in 1975, it "suspended research with human subjects."[9]

This secrecy surrounding the horrific aspects of World War II has
allowed the sanitized version to persist and has impacted the view of subsequent wars and their warriors, often to the detriment of the younger
veterans. Vietnam veterans, in particular, tell of returning from their war
and listening to the statements of some World War II veterans in this
vein, "I was in WWII, the big one, and I do not have any problems from
my war." Joe "Ragman" Tarnovsky, a Vietnam vet, wrote an article for
Veterans Today disputing the accuracy of that statement. "Ragman" posits
that those World War II veterans who deny having any aftereffects of
combat were men who saw little or no combat. "Ragman," a combat vet

8. Susan L. Smith, "Mustard Gas and American Race-Based Experimentation in World War II," *Journal of Law, Medicine and Ethics* 36(3), Fall 2008, 517–21.
9. Smith, 521, fn 5.

himself, felt that for "combat soldiers from any war, the horrendous sight and smell of death and having to participate in the taking of human lives will leave mental and emotional wounds." This Vietnam veteran faults the government and media for not making public the knowledge that World War II combat vets were suffering. He points to Audie Murphy as a prime example. Murphy actually went public with his postwar trauma in the hope that it would help soldiers after him. However, since Murphy's honesty did not fit in with the prevailing ethos of the stoic World War II warrior, the war's emotional cost to him was not a big news story. "Ragman" feels that his generation of soldiers would have benefited had they known "that the most decorated American soldier had once faced a murder charge, was acquitted, slept with a loaded gun by his bed, and had held his first wife at gunpoint . . . maybe those of us with PTSD would have felt we were not crazy . . . even heroes can be affected by their combat experience."[10]

Our newest veterans would also benefit from a more thorough understanding of their grandfathers' return from World War II. In *Lethal Warrior: When the New Band of Brothers Came Home—Uncovering the Tragic Reality of PTSD,* journalist David Phillips reported on the return of the 4th Brigade Combat Team to Fort Carson, Colorado. During the brigade's two tours in Iraq, they took many casualties, one hundred killed and five hundred wounded. When these warriors came home, Colorado Springs warmly welcomed them back with parades and yellow ribbons. Imagine the community's shock when, after a year home, nine soldiers from the unit had been arrested for random and senseless murders. After all, weren't the lessons from World War II and Vietnam that if our boys came home from battle to parades and thank you's they would not suffer from war trauma? The town seemed under the impression "that all that was needed to diffuse the explosive emotions of war and save a new generation of soldiers from alcoholism, drugs, despondency, and post-traumatic stress disorder was a really emphatic thank you."[11]

---

10. Joe "Ragman" Tarnovsky, "PTSD, If We Had Only Known About Audie Murphy" *Veterans Today: Military & Foreign Affairs Journal,* June 15, 2010, accessed, August 15, 2010, http://www.veteranstoday.com/2010/06/15/joe-ragman-tarnovsky-ptsd-if-we-had-only-known-about-audie-murphy.

11. David Philipps, *Lethal Warriors: When the New Band of Brothers Came Home—Uncovering the Tragic Reality of PTSD* (New York: Palgrave-Macmillan, 2010), 92–93.

By separating our wars into good and bad and dividing generations of soldiers, pitting them against each other as tough or weak based on their supposed handling of war trauma, a huge disservice has been done to all our warriors. Dr. Raymond Scurfield, a Vietnam veteran, has studied the universality of war both in leading therapy groups and in his books. Scurfield, who knows war firsthand, has wise advice. Veterans of different eras should share and interact with each other to reach the awareness that "beyond the uniqueness of each era and theater of war, there is also a universality of the experience of war and its social and psychological impact."[12]

12. Raymond M. Scurfield, *War Trauma: Lesson Unlearned from Vietnam to Iraq* (New York" Algora Publishing, 2006), 181.

ABOUT THE AUTHOR

CAROL SCHULTZ VENTO is a former Political Science professor and an attorney. She received her undergraduate degree in Sociology, Master's degree in Public Administration, and doctorate in Political Science from Temple University. Her law degree is from Rutgers University School of Law. She is the daughter of World War II veteran Arthur 'Dutch' Schultz, the 82nd Airborne paratrooper portrayed in the 1962 D-Day movie *The Longest Day* by Richard Beymer. Dutch's war experiences have also been written about in a number of books about the European Theater in World War II, including those by Stephen Ambrose and Patrick O'Donnell. Carol is a native of Philadelphia and currently lives in Palmyra, New Jersey with her husband Frank.

Find Carol Schultz Vento at:

Facebook: (1) Carol Schultz Vento, Author; (2) DaughtersofD-Day
Instagram: csvento
Twitter/X: @ddaydaughter